Eco Kids

**SELF-SUFFICIENCY
HANDBOOK**

Eco Kids

SELF-SUFFICIENCY
HANDBOOK

ALAN & GILL
BRIDGEWATER

NEW
HOLLAND

First published in 2009 by
New Holland Publishers (UK) Ltd
London • Cape Town • Sydney • Auckland

Garfield House
86–88 Edgware Road
London, W2 2EA
United Kingdom
www.newhollandpublishers.com

80 McKenzie Street
Cape Town 8001
South Africa

Unit 1, 66 Gibbes Street
Chatswood, NSW 2067
Australia

218 Lake Road
Northcote, Auckland
New Zealand

Copyright © 2009 text: A. & G. Bridgewater
Copyright © 2009 photographs and illustrations:
New Holland Publishers (UK) Ltd
Copyright © 2009 New Holland Publishers (UK) Ltd

10 9 8 7 6 5 4 3 2 1

ISBN 978 1 84773 439 6

Editors: **Amy Corstorphine and Alison Copland**
Design: **AG&G Books**
Production: **Laurence Poos**
Editorial Direction: **Rosemary Wilkinson**
Additional photos: **IStock Photo**

Reproduction by PDQ Media Solutions, Ltd, UK
Printed and bound by Times Offset, Malaysia

A big thank you to the children:
**Charlotte Roberts, Hamish Roberts,
Isobel Roberts, Terri Hill, Harley Bridgewater**
and **Jessica Bridgewater**

Thanks also to the students of **Esher School** for the
Carry Freedom trailer photos on pages 93-95

Contents

Introduction

What is 'eco kids' self-sufficiency'?

If as a kid you can do things like build a camp, light a fire, cook out in the open, sleep under the stars, mend your bike, grow your own vegetables and keep chickens for eggs, then you are well on the way to becoming independent, or 'self-sufficient', which means you don't have to rely on other

people. Where it gets really exciting is that, if you can build a self-sufficient world in miniature, then when you are older you will be able to confidently shape and build your adult world.

Why should we care about the environment?

If you imagine yourself travelling out into space and looking down at our world from a distance, you'll see that all the things we know – our homes, families, friends, food, forests, animals, rivers and seas – are down here on Earth. If we believe just a little bit of what we read and see on the TV, and if we take it as fact that our 'Mother Earth' is sick, stressed out and generally very unhappy, then it's plain to see that we must begin to look after our wildlife, care for our plants, reduce pollution and generally tidy up our way of living. Think about it – if Mother Earth is all we have, and there's nowhere else to go, we simply have no other choice than to look after our environment very carefully.

How you can help improve the world

First things first – there's no need for you to get stressed and anxious about eco issues. Things like pollution are important and real, and we do need to make huge changes, but the fact that these problems are real means that we can use muscle-and-brain solutions to sort them out. In the same way as you can keep your bedroom clean by taking off your shoes before you enter it – so that the floor doesn't get covered in muddy footprints – we all need to make a number of small changes so that we move through everyday life without leaving a line of filthy, waste-covered, pollution-smeared, carbon-heavy 'footprints'.

If you show your friends that your den is not only a fun adventure, but also an ongoing mission to explore eco-green issues such as growing food, recycling and generally being self-sufficient, then you are in a way showing your friends how it's possible to care for the whole world. Your self-sufficient, 'eco-warrior' efforts will set off a chain reaction that will eventually change things for the better.

SAFETY ADVICE FOR ADULTS AND CHILDREN
READ THIS BEFORE STARTING A PROJECT
Adults must not allow children to use stepladders, dangerous tools or be near dangerous structures and hazardous conditions. We recommend that children only be allowed to use a hammer, a handsaw and a CORDLESS drill/driver and ONLY when a loving, caring and responsible adult is supervising them. Adults using tools and ladders must follow the manufacturer's instructions for safe operation (wear a dust mask and eye protection if instructed to do so). Adults must not operate dangerous power tools with children nearby. Every project has a safety rating indicated by the following symbols.

 ASK AN ADULT TO HELP: the project uses dangerous tools; an adult must do the dangerous bits and kids must be supervised at all times.

 BE CAREFUL: the project needs adult supervision at all times.

 ALWAYS ASK: kids should check with an adult before using the tools and materials.

How to use tools safely and properly

First read the safety advice on page 9. The most important points to remember are not to allow children to use dangerous tools and always follow the tool manufacturers' operating instructions. Below is a list of tools used and how to use them safely and effectively.

COMPASSES: A two-legged tool used for scribing and marking circles and radii. In use fix the legs a set distance apart, spike one leg down on the workpiece, and then scribe the arc, circle or step-off.

CORDLESS DRILL/DRIVER: Used for drilling holes and driving in screws. Safe (low voltage) and good for remote locations. For drilling, set the tool to drilling mode, fit the appropriate drill bit and drill the hole ensuring your free hand is away from the drill bit. For small holes use twist bits and for large holes (above 10 mm) use flat bits. For driving in screws, set the tool to screwing mode and the lowest speed and choose a torque setting. The torque setting (numbers dialled by rotating the end "chuck" of the tool) is a function to avoid over tightening the screws; a low number uses very little power for small screws and a high number uses more power for larger screws. The tool stops driving and starts clicking when the torque setting has been applied.

DARNING NEEDLE: A blunt ended needle with a big eye used with thick thread for hand sewing. In use yarn or thread is passed through the eye and the needle is threaded in and out of the fabric.

GARDENING TROWEL: A small hand-held digging tool. Used for digging small holes in soil.

HAMMER: Used for driving in pins and nails. A claw on the back of the hammer is used for extracting nails. The nail is held between finger and thumb, and gently tapped with the hammerhead until the nail supports itself, the supporting hand is then removed and the nail is driven home.

HAND-AXE: Used to shape wood. **Do not allow children to use this tool.** In use, the tool is held in one hand and swung so the blade cuts the wood.

HANDSAW: A general purpose saw for cutting straight lines in wood. The saw is held with one hand, the blade is aligned with the cut line and is pushed and pulled.

JIGSAW: A powered saw with a thin blade for cutting straight lines and curves in thin-section wood. **Do not allow children to use this tool.** In action, the blade is aligned with the line of cut, the power is switched on and the tool is advanced.

KITCHEN KNIFE: Used for cutting insulation board. A saw-toothed knife is a safer option. Held in one hand and used like a saw.

KNITTING NEEDLE: Used in pairs for knitting wool. Choose the right size of needle for the thickness of wool. In use, the needles are held one in each hand and are used to hook and knot the wool.

MEZZALUNA: A two-handed knife used for chopping herbs and so on. Inherently safe as it is held with both hands. In use the tool is held with both hands and the food is cut with a chopping, rocking motion.

PAINTBRUSH: Used for applying paint and varnish. Instructions for using paint and cleaning brushes are found on the paint tin.

SANDPAPER: Abrasive paper used for smoothing wood. In use, the paper is supported on the hand or around a block and worked back and forth in a scrubbing motion.

SEWING-MACHINE: Used for sewing fabrics. Follow the manufacturers' instructions.

SLEDGEHAMMER: A long handled heavy hammer for banging in posts, breaking rubble and compacting earth. **Do not allow children to use this tool.** In use, the handle is gripped in both hands and the tool is swung so the head strikes the post, rubble or earth.

SPADE: Use for digging holes in the ground. In use the handle is held and manoeuvred by both hands, the metal blade is positioned where you want to dig and one foot is used to push down on the top of the blade.

SPANNER: Used for adjusting nuts and bolts. Choose a spanner to fit the nut or bolt, place it on the nut or bolt and rotate to loosen or tighten.

SPIRIT LEVEL: A testing tool to check your work is horizontal or vertical. The absolute level is indicated by the bubble. In use, the tool is positioned on the workpiece at which point the workpiece is adjusted until the bubble is centred between two lines.

STEPLADDER: A portable ladder consisting of a hinged frame with a small platform at the top. Has to be placed on a firm, level surface. **Do not allow children to use a stepladder.** In use, the ladder is opened, positioned and set level.

TAPE-MEASURE: Flexible steel, retractable ruler used for measuring. Another fabric version is used for sewing projects. In use, the zero end is positioned, the tape-measure is extended along the workpiece and a mark is made or a measurement is taken.

TRY-SQUARE: Use for testing lines and edges are at right angles (90°) to each other. In use, the wooden stock is held hard up against the edge of the workpiece and a line is drawn along the edge of the steel blade.

T-SQUARE: Similar to a try-square but much larger.

WHEELBARROW: A one-wheeled cart used for moving soil and other heavy loads. In use, the barrow is filled, the handles are lifted and the barrow is pushed along. The contents can be tipped out of the front.

ECO DEN

About eco dens

An eco den is a sort of mix-up between an old shack in the woods, a small gypsy caravan, a canal boat, a tree-house and a self-contained space pod. The aim is to build a self-sufficient hideout using mostly recycled materials – a place where you and your mates can hang out and do your own thing. An adult will need to help you with this project.

How about this for a good eco den?

ECO TIPS

What does it mean to be 'self-sufficient'?

A truly self-sufficient set-up – a home, village, town or city – would produce all its own food, swap things, create its own energy, and clean up its own waste.

Melting sea ice is a threat to the polar bear because it reduces its ability to find food

What does 'off-grid' mean?

An off-grid house – it could be your den – finds its own water and creates its own energy without tapping into the normal, 'on-grid' supplies of water, gas, oil and electricity. An off-grid home uses non-fossil energy such as wind and solar power.

Why is it important to reuse and recycle?

Reusing or recycling as many things as possible keeps goods and materials out of our waste dumps, which are rapidly becoming full up. Because we then don't need so many new things, it also saves energy, reduces the strain on natural resources, creates less pollution, saves money and generally makes for a much more clean and comfortable life for everyone.

Most of our waste metal, plastic and paper could be recycled

What has recycling got to do with a den?

'Eco' or 'eco-friendly' means doing things in a way that doesn't hurt nature, and 'recycling' means converting unwanted materials into something new, so an eco den is built using 'salvaged' (found) or recycled materials in a way that doesn't damage the environment. We used an old window, left-over paint, a mixture of left-over and salvaged wood, and other 'rubbish' that would otherwise have been wasted.

Can a den be completely off-grid?

The off-grid bit will really depend upon where you live, and on how much time and effort you're going to put in. We have built a rain-collector for water, as well as a wind turbine and a solar panel for lights, but we also have to go back to the house for some water, and to use the toilet. You also might like to build a solar oven for simple cooking.

How different can your den be?

Your den can be very different from ours. The shape will be decided by your found shed, and its character will be shaped by the colour, the size, the nature of your salvaged materials, and your interests. Bigger, smaller, lower, higher, with more windows, a different roof, a bigger porch – your den can be anything that takes your fancy.

Will an eco den cost lots of money?

If you look in your local newspaper, you'll see that there are lots of old sheds free for collection. Our shed was a complete mess – every wall and floor panel was in some way broken. All we did was patch it up with thrown-away materials. The biggest costs were for the metal sheets for the roof, and for the hundreds of screws and nails.

Why is an eco den so good?

First of all, an eco den is fun, exciting and challenging to build. When finished, it's cosy and private and it's a place where you can hang out with your mates or invite them for a sleep-over. It's good for quiet reading and for doing your homework – basically it's a place where you can do exactly what you want, when you want.

How to build your own eco den

Ask an adult to help

You need...

- An old shed
- Salvaged concrete blocks or slabs
- Tape measure and spirit level
- Slab, tile or slate for packing pieces
- Joists about 10 x 10 cm (4 x 4 in)
- Roofing felt
- Screws, nails, fencing staples and roofing screws, sizes and quantity to fit your salvaged materials
- Cordless drill/driver and bits
- Hammer
- Salvaged wood for repairs and additions (depending on your shed condition and design)
- Handsaw
- 2 G-clamps
- Chicken wire, enough to wrap around the base of the shed once
- Ladder
- Insulation board, enough to cover the roof and the walls
- Roof battens (thin sticks of wood) 4 x 2 cm (1 ½ x ¾ in), enough to cover your roof at 46 cm (18 in) intervals
- Salvaged plastic window
- Corrugated metal roofing sheet, enough to cover the roof with approximately 7 cm (3 in) overlaps and in a length that overhangs your shed by at least 10 cm (4 in)
- Metal roofing ridge strip, enough to cover your shed with approximately 7 cm (3 in) overlaps
- Sealant
- Left-over paint and paintbrushes
- Wheelbarrow

Some ideas for customizing your den

'Lean-to' for storage

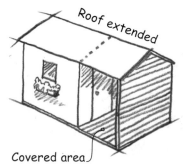

Roof extended

Covered area

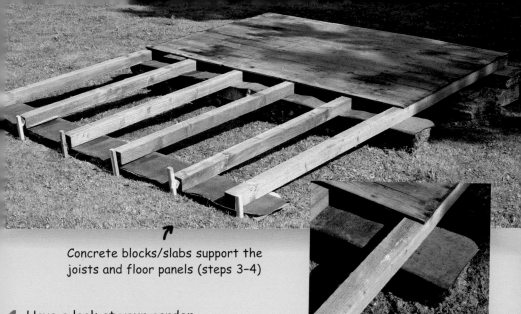

Concrete blocks/slabs support the joists and floor panels (steps 3–4)

Put roofing felt between the blocks/slabs and the joists (step 4)

1 Have a look at your garden and talk to your family, then ask yourself what sort of den you are aiming for. Also, where is the den going to be built?

2 Search for a shed that you like and dismantle into panels. Measure the length and width of your shed. If it's going on a level, paved patio then you can miss out the next step.

3 Set concrete blocks/slabs directly on the ground at each corner so that they match up with the size and shape of your shed floor panel(s). Check your layout has 90° corners by measuring the diagonals with a tape measure (the distance between opposite corners). Make adjustments until both diagonals

are equal. If you fail to achieve 90° corners the shed will be skewed and crooked. Place more blocks at regular intervals for supporting the joists – these are strong pieces of wood, about 10 x 10 cm (4 x 4 in), that support all the weight, and they need to be spaced about 40 cm (16 in) apart. Use 'packing pieces' (slab, tile or slate) laid on top of the blocks/slabs to make them level with each other (use a spirit level to check, see page 11 for how to do this).

4 Lay out the joists and slide pieces of roofing felt between the wooden joists and the blocks/slabs to stop damp.

Support the wood at a convenient height and get someone to hold it down firmly as you saw (step 7)

Add corner trim (step 9)

5 Lift the floor panels into place and fix them with screws or nails. This is heavy and tricky, so you'll need help.

6 Using the level floor panels as a workbench, put the wall panels down on it and use a hammer to remove rotten wood and remove any rusty nails.

7 Measure the lengths of wood that need replacing. Transfer the measurements through to the new wood and use the saw to cut them to size. Nail the 'patches' carefully in place. Be careful to avoid hurting your hands on splinters and sharp nails.

8 If you need to mend the frame, cut out the rotten bits, cut new bits to fit in the gaps and screw them in place. Use extra bits of wood to bridge across the mends.

9 Use G-clamps to fix the position of the four wall panels in place on the floor panel, and carefully screw them firmly to the floor and to each other. Add battens ('trim') to the four outside corners of the shed.

10 Use chicken wire wrapped around the base of the shed, stapled in place and buried 30 cm (12 in) in the ground to prevent animals from burrowing under the shed.

11 You'll need help to lift the roof panels in place – make sure they are well located and aligned and fix them with screws driven through into the top edge of the wall. Screw adjoining roof panels together at the ridge (from inside the shed).

Roof detail (step 12)

12 Carefully cut the insulation to fit, cover the insulation with the roofing felt and fix with roof battens nailed securely to the roof as seen in the photo above.

13 Here, a plastic window found on a skip was used to replace the broken window. Fix with screws.

Install the window (step 13)

14 We decided to extend the roof and make an area of decking at the front by removing the turf, placing extra joists level with the floor of the shed, decking the joists, and using posts and battens to create a support structure for the added roof. The main part of this structure is an 'A'-frame which is the same shape as the roof. Join the bits of wood with screws or nails and then cut to length as shown in the picture opposite.

Extending the roof (step 14)

15 Screw the corrugated roofing sheets in place using roofing screws.

16 Fix a metal ridge strip to cover the join at the top of the roof using roofing screws.

Adding the finishing touch to the roof (step 16)

17 Add other decorative details to your shed in whatever way you like. We added a rustic balustrade and decking at the front but you could take inspiration from the materials you have salvaged.

Finish off the den ↱
with left-over paint
(step 18)

18 Finally, when you have finished applying decorative details seal any gaps with sealant (partcularly around the window). Paint the walls and doors inside and out in the colours of your choice (we used odds and ends of left-over paint). Look out for some chairs and extra furniture.

Decorate the inside of the den however you like!

Insulation

If you miss out a layer of insulation, your den will be icy cold in winter and baking hot in summer. You will then have to waste loads of money on either heating or cooling it so that it is nice to spend time in.

What can you use to insulate your den?

You can line the walls inside your den with fibreglass loft insulation (always wearing a mask, overalls and gloves) or insulation board. You can also use old woollen blankets, corrugated cardboard or straw, covered with thin sheets of recycled plywood. If your window isn't double-glazed, why not have thick curtains? Keep icy blasts out with a long, sausage-shaped pillow at the bottom of the door (stuff old trouser legs with rags, and then tie the ends round with string).

Cut the insulation board to size

Cover all the walls with insulation

Cover the insulation with plywood

26

ECO TIPS

Why is insulation so important?

Insulating materials such as wool, fibreglass, compressed paper and processed plant fibres are winners on two counts – they are less expensive than high-cost energy, and their use saves more energy. The more insulation you have, the more money you save.

Sheep's wool and grass

When it comes to insulation and saving energy, the very best option would be to wrap your house up in wool and bury it in the ground under a layer of living grass. You can't get warmer or cooler than that, because wool and grass are both excellent insulating materials.

Its wool keeps a sheep warm in winter and cool in summer

This underground house is perfectly insulated

Picnic table

This project is great because it only uses recycled wood. The posts came from a pile of wood we had put aside for logs, the top was an old door we found washed up on a beach, and the seat boards were a pair of offcuts from the local sawmill. Before you start, ask an adult to help you with this project. The wood is quite heavy and tools like the hand-axe are very dangerous so must only be used by an adult.

A broken and damaged forest
is a sad and ugly sight

What is deforestation?

Deforestation is the destruction, clearing and removal of our forests. This
kills wildlife, reduces oxygen, damages the soil, pollutes the atmosphere,
causes flooding, and generally messes up our world.

Is it important to reuse and recycle wood?

Yes – reusing and recycling wood will help to slow down deforestation. The
more paper we recycle, the more solid wood we recycle and/or use as fuel,
and the more we stop sawing down trees, the longer our forests will last.

Where can you find free wood?

Of course it depends on where you live, but you could perhaps try a river
or a beach for **driftwood**, shops that sell motorcycles for **packing cases**,
sawmills for **sawn offcuts** or a local builder who may have non-returnable
pallets and **old wood or offcuts** to dispose of. Always check that it's OK
to salvage the wood, and watch for any sharp nails sticking out!

How to make the picnic table

You need...

▷ Salvaged door to make a tabletop about 210 cm (82 in) long, 75 cm (30 in) wide, with two seats about 220 cm (87 in) long, 30 cm (12 in) wide

▷ 4 sticks for marking out

▷ Spade

▷ Green wood (with bark on it): 8 poles each at 254 cm (100 in) long

▷ Tape measure

▷ Handsaw and hand-axe

▷ Hammer and 15 cm (6 in) nails

Lay all the parts out on the grass (step 1)

Nail the long bars to the posts (step 2)

1 Lay your found tabletop on the grass where you want the table, mark its position with four sticks, and start by digging 8 holes in the ground, 30 cm (12 in) deep for the vertical posts. The seat post holes need to be 53 cm (21 in) away from the table leg posts. Cut 4 table leg posts 102 cm (40 in) long, and 4 seat posts 66 cm (26 in) long.

2 Set the eight posts in the ground – 4 at each end – replace earth around the poles and use your foot to stomp the earth down. Measure and carefully cut horizontal bars to fit across the posts and nail them in place as shown. The lengths of these bars will vary dramatically depending on your materials.

Cut flat areas to make a good fit (step 3)

3 When you're working with poles, always make sure when nailing one part to another that they come right together for a good, close fit. Use the handsaw and hand-axe (remember only adults must use the hand-axe) to create some flat areas so that the logs will fit together snugly.

Make sure the seat is level (step 4)

4 Bridge the tabletop and seat planks over the horizontal bars and nail in place. Nail the seat planks in place at either side of the table.

5 Fix each seat plank so the straightest edge is facing the table. This is so the sitters can sit down without scratching the back of their legs.

More picnic-table ideas

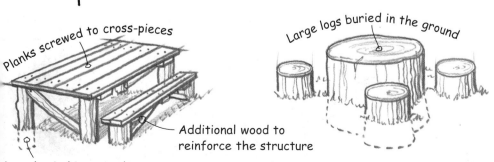

Planks screwed to cross-pieces

Large logs buried in the ground

Additional wood to reinforce the structure

Legs buried in ground

Knitted bedspread

The greatest thing about our lovely knitted patchwork bedspread is that it's totally eco-friendly. It's completely handmade (no carbon-producing machines or motors are needed), it uses loads of recycled wool, and, best of all, once finished it will keep you really warm as well as looking pretty. It's fun to make and to use!

s knitting easy?

Basic hand knitting is very easy. All you need is the wool or yarn, a pair of knitting needles and a few basic tips, and you'll be well away. The best way of learning is to have one-to-one lessons – someone in your family will most likely be a first-class knitter. Here are some interesting facts and figures to think about:

* **Knitting was once a macho activity** – the sort of thing that soldiers and sailors did between battles.
* **Knitting helps the brain work** – it's good for maths and for eye-and-hand coordination.
* **There are over 24 million keen knitters in the USA alone** – so how many do you think there might be in the whole world?

How to knit your own bedspread

?
Always ask

You need...

▷ Left-over wool
▷ Pair of 4 mm (US 6) knitting needles
▷ Tape measure
▷ Scissors
▷ Large darning needle
▷ Thread

How to knit

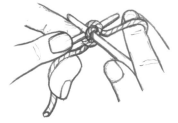

CASTING ON Make a loop on the left hand needle and knot loosely to secure. This is the first stitch. Pull through a stitch on the left needle and slip the new loop/stitch onto the left needle.

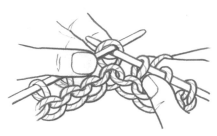

THE KNIT STITCH 1 Insert the poin of the right needle into the stitch on the left needle.

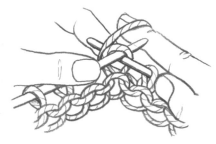

THE KNIT STITCH 2 With your index finger, wind the yarn under and over the point of the right needle.

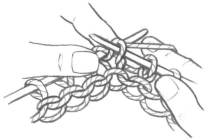

THE KNIT STITCH 3 Using the right needle, pull the new stitch through the old stitch to form a loop, and slide the old stitch off the left needle onto the right needle.

1 Search for left-over wool – try charity shops, friends and family. It's best if the wool is all the same weight and thickness.

2 Find someone who knows how to knit, and ask them to show you a few basic stitches, as well as how to start or 'cast on', and how to finish off.

Ask a good knitter to help

3 Once you can manage a stitch, practise over and over again until you know what you are doing.

4 When you and your mates have knitted a big stack of rectangles – we used 104 rectangles each measuring 25 x 18 cm (10 x 7 in) (60 sts, 48 rows) – then you can start sewing them together using a simple back stitch (see page 122) into strips.

5 Finally, once you have sewn 13 rectangles end-to-end to make eight strips, and the eight strips side-to-side to make the blanket, ask an adult to sew a hem all around the blanket to give it strength.

Practising the knit stitch →

A team effort! ↘

Adirondack chair

Ask an adult
to help

An Adirondack chair is a comfortable outdoor chair that you can easily make from recycled wood. It was originally a sort of roughly built chair, homemade by poor people in the Adirondack Mountains region of the USA. Next time you see a film that shows American mountain folk sitting around on a porch, have a close-up look at the chairs – they could well be Adirondacks.

Drawings to help make the chair

We have noted the important dimensions (but all the other sizes will depend on what pieces of wood you can find)

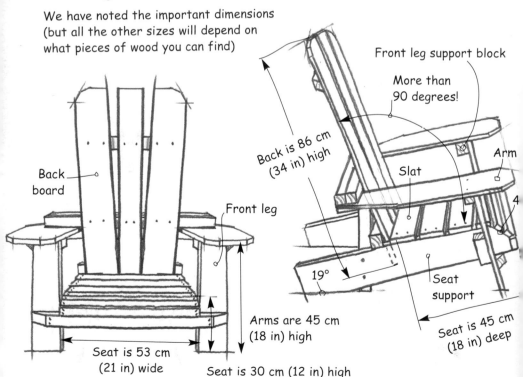

Back board

Front leg

Front leg support block

More than 90 degrees!

Back is 86 cm (34 in) high

Slat

Arm

19°

Seat support

Arms are 45 cm (18 in) high

Seat is 53 cm (21 in) wide

Seat is 30 cm (12 in) high

Seat is 45 cm (18 in) deep

How to make the chair

You need...

▷ Salvaged planks and sticks.
The largest you need are 87 cm
(34 in) long and 15 cm (6 in)
wide). Other sizes are noted in
the instructions below.

▷ Handsaw

▷ Tape measure and pencil

▷ Cordless drill/driver, bits and
screws

▷ Sandpaper, left-over paint and
paintbrush

Screw the back legs to the
seat supports (step 2)

1 Cut two seat supports 76 cm
(30 in) long, 23 cm (9 in) wide
that tapers off to 18 cm (7 in) at
the front. Cut a 45° angle off the
front ends and a 19° angle off the
back ends as shown in the drawing.
Bridge the seat supports with
54 cm (21 in) long slats of varying
widths (whatever is available) and
screw them in place.

2 Cut two front leg support
blocks 15 cm (6 in) long from
5 x 5 cm (2 x 2 in) sized wood and
screw them to the seat supports
15 cm (6 in) from the front. Cut
two vertical supports for the back
of the chair 37 cm (14¹/₂ in) from
5 x 5 cm (2 x 2 in) sized wood and
screw them to the inside of the

seat supports about 43 cm (17 in)
from the back (as shown in the
photo above).

3 Make the back from three
boards 12-15 cm (5-6 in) wide
and 87 cm (34 in) long. Cut angles
off the tops of two of the boards
as shown in the drawing on page 36.
Arrange them in a flared shape,
(also shown on page 34) but the
exact shape is not critical. Join
them using screws with one stick
26 cm (10 in) from the top and
another stick 54 cm (21 in) set
13 cm (5 in) from the bottom).

Screw the boards to the sticks (step 3)

4 Make the frame as shown in the picture below. The front legs are 47 cm (18½ in) long and 15 cm (6 in) wide. The arms are 66 cm (26 in) long and 23 cm (9 in) wide. The arms and legs are spaced 54 cm (21 in) apart and linked by 84 cm (33 in)- long horizontal rails at the front and back, screwed in place. The front legs are joined to the arms using support blocks and screws as shown in the diagram on page 36.

5 Rest the seat on the rail that links the two front legs, slide the back piece down between the arms and the seat, and screw the three parts together.

6 Smooth off any splinters and sharp edges using sandpaper, and then paint the whole chair in a colour (or colours) of your choice.

Ask all your friends to help (step 4)

ECO FOOD

Herbs and salad crops

Have you ever grown your own salad?

Growing your own food is one of those really amazing back-to-basics experiences that just shouldn't be missed. It's great fun – watching the plants develop, fighting off insects and bugs, harvesting – and then at the end of it all wolfing it down.

Using the windowsill

?

Always ask

This is a good idea if you don't have any outdoor space. You'll find that you can grow a surprising range of food crops on a windowsill. The easiest option is to go for fast-growing items like pick-and-eat salads, radishes, chives and herbs. You could find a ready-made windowbox, or make your own out of recycled materials, or you could just put up a shelf strong enough to take a row of recycled pots and tubs (see below), or even some old buckets or paint tins.

See how many recycled containers you can find to use

Building a wall planter

We built our planter with five short lengths of wood that we salvaged from a pallet, and an armful of split logs. We just screwed the planks together to make the box, and then fixed the logs with more screws.

Use a mezzaluna to chop herbs so that you can't cut your hand →

Giant salad sandwiches are good for you!

43

Runner beans

You start with a few seeds and very soon you've got plenty of lush green beans.

It's an adventure – thinking about the variety to grow, watching the plants develop, building a support 'wigwam', fighting off harmful insects and bugs, harvesting, and then at the end of it all having plate after plate piled high with beautiful, tasty runner beans.

How to grow runner beans in a dumpy bag

You need...

▷ Offcut length of blue plastic pipe long enough to make a hoop to fit the bag and a 13 cm (5 in) length of "broomstick" dowel.

▷ Handsaw

▷ Dumpy bag – the sort of bag used by builders' merchants

▷ Wooden pallet

▷ Spent mushroom compost

▷ Pot-grown runner-bean seedlings

▷ 8 strong sticks made from a wood species like beech and a ball of strong string

Push the two ends so that they come together on the wooden 'broomstick' dowel (step 1)

1 Cut the plastic tube to length so that it makes a hoop that is a tight fit in the neck of the bag. Bang the length of 'broomstick' dowel into one end of the tube and use it to join the two ends together to make a hoop.

2 Sit the dumpy bag on the pallet, and start to fill it with the compost. When the bag is about half full, put the hoop over the outside of the bag and fold the top of the bag over on itself so that the hoop is covered. Add more compost until the bag starts to bulge and the hoop is held in place.

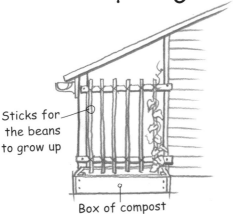

Fold the edges of the bulging bag down over the hoop (step 2)

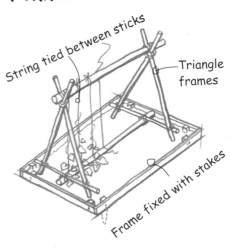

Plant the seedlings about 23–30 cm (9-12 in) apart (step 3)

More ways to grow runner beans

Sticks for the beans to grow up

Box of compost

String tied between sticks

Triangle frames

Frame fixed with stakes

3 Stamp the compost down until it's firm. Plant the seedlings in 8 cm (3 in) deep holes in the compost about 23–30 cm (9–12 in) apart. Water well.

4 Once the plants start to grow strongly, put the sticks around the bag to make a 'wigwam' frame for the beans to grow around. Make sure you sink the sticks well into the ground and tie the sticks together at the top with strong string.

The wigwam must be well fixed (step 4)

Why is organic good?

Organic food is free from all the harmful chemicals that poison the land, wildlife and us. Organic food might look a bit bumpy and lumpy, but it tastes, smells and feels good.

Growing your own and buying locally

Growing your own food and/or buying it in your local area cuts down on packaging, transport costs and pollution.

Food packaging: the pros and cons

PROS
* Reduces physical damage
* Makes it easier to transport
* Increases shelf-life

CONS
* Increases transport costs
* Wasteful in raw materials
* Makes it difficult for us to inspect the food before buying
* Makes it difficult to present food that is in any way unusually big, small or bendy
* Increases waste

Potatoes

Have you ever eaten your own spuds?

Growing your own potatoes is really exciting. You put in a dozen wrinkly old 'seed potatoes', and these turn into bucketfuls of smooth, shiny, tasty spuds. Of course digging them up is good fun, a bit like hunting for buried treasure, but best of all is eating them.

How to grow potatoes

Sew the rolled-over edge of the bag to the hoop (step 2)

You need...

▷ Offcut length of blue plastic pipe long enough to make a hoop to fit the bag and a 13 cm (5 in) length of 'broomstick' dowel

▷ Dumpy bag

▷ Wooden pallet

▷ Spent mushroom compost

▷ 4 iron hook-ended fence stakes

▷ Strong plastic rope, 8 m (26ft) long

▷ Large darning needle and some thin nylon string

▷ Sprouting seed potatoes

1 Prepare the dumpy bag as in steps 1 and 2 of the bean project (see pages 44 and 46).

2 Push the iron fence stakes into the ground – one at each 'corner' of the bag. Use rope to tie the bag loops to the top of the stakes. Use the needle and nylon string to sew the edge over the hoop.

3 Plant the seed potatoes so that they are about 23–30 cm (9–12 in) apart and 7.5–15 cm (3–6 in) deep and then just sit back and wait for them to grow.

4 When the leaves and flowers fade, the new potatoes are ready to be dug up. To cook them, first wash off all the earth, and boil them for 20–30 minutes. You can then pile them high up on your plate, dribble them with butter or olive oil, cover them with baked beans and start eating.

↑
Plant the seed potatoes about 23–30 cm (9–12 in) apart (step 3)

Digging up your new spuds is cool!

Tomatoes

Home-grown tomatoes might be funny shapes and a bit small, but they taste simply wonderful. These days shop-bought, non-organic tomatoes seem to be just big, tasteless bags of nothing, which is not really surprising because most aren't grown in soil or compost at all, but in chemical baths. For the real taste of tomatoes, you need to grow your own – then you'll know the difference!

How to grow your own tomatoes

You need...

▷ A 5–7.5 cm (2–3 in) deep seed-tray or found box

▷ Fine rich compost or the compost from tomato grow-bags

▷ Tomato seeds – an outdoor 'bush' variety

▷ Sheet of clear perspex and some newspaper

▷ 12 x 7.5–13 cm (3–5 in) pots or found containers

▷ Liquid tomato feed (see page 51)

▷ Hanging basket or other container

1 Fill the seed-tray with the fine rich compost, remove any stones or bits and gently firm it level with your hands. Sprinkle the seeds over the compost, and cover them with a further thin layer of compost. Water with a fine spray, and cover the tray with a sheet of perspex topped with newspaper. Leave in a sheltered, sunny spot.

2 Two weeks or so after sowing the seeds, take the young seedlings one at a time from the tray and plant them in the 12 pots, filled with more compost.

3 Water the plants, give them a small liquid feed, and transfer them to a warm, sheltered spot.

4 When the plants are so big that they look as if they're going to jump out of their pots, carefully remove them and plant them into the much larger hanging pots or containers.

The red ones are ready to eat (step 5)

5 Finally, keep watering and feeding until the tomatoes look ready to be picked.

Dribble the feed onto the compost, not the leaves (step 3)

Liquid feed for tomatoes

Find a pair of old tights and stuff them full with fresh sheep or horse poo. Submerge it in a dustbin full of water and leave to soak for 4–6 weeks. When your tomato plants start to bear fruit, give them increasingly bigger and bigger drinks of this liquid poo feed.

Poo is good for something! →

Chickens and eggs

Chickens don't just lay eggs – they are also great fun to watch! They chase and fight each other for tasty snacks like worms, flies, beetles and bugs, save time by peeing and pooing from the same hole, and enjoy nothing more than 'bathing' in dusty holes in the ground. After a hard day's work they perch precariously on a stick or tree branch and go to sleep.

Sometimes you need to help the mother hen look after the chicks

Feeding a tame cockerel (male chicken)

Young chicks keep warm by snuggling underneath the mother hen

ECO TIPS

What are 'battery chickens'?

A battery chicken or hen spends all its life in a small wire cage, standing on crippled legs and feet on a space no bigger than a sheet of typing paper.

Why is chicken meat so cheap?

Battery-bred chicken meat is cheap because the system keeps costs down by treating the hen as a product, like baked beans. If the hen is ill or doesn't lay, it is killed.

What does 'free-range' mean?

A truly free-range chicken is free to roam and live its life in a field – it can run, flap, peck, eat insects and generally do what chickens enjoy doing.

This poor battery hen has spent its whole life standing in a cage

These lucky free-range chickens are free to enjoy life

What have chickens got to do with eco self-sufficiency?

The best way of getting a really good egg – fresh, tasty and free from additives – is to keep your own chickens. Even better, when you're feeding your kitchen scraps to the chickens and eating your own eggs rather than shop-bought ones, you're cutting down on food waste and all the packaging and transport that is needed for shop-bought goods. Keeping chickens is an all-round eco winner!

Can you make a chicken house from recycled materials?

You can make a chicken house from just about any mix of materials that will keep the chickens warm and dry in the winter, and cool and fresh in the summer. We made ours from bits of plywood, waterproof plastic, battens and such like – materials left over from making the eco den (see pages 18–25). You could make yours from an old shed, a wooden packing case, a frame covered in roof felt and tin – in fact anything you can knock together to make a little hut.

Are chickens easy to keep?

If you give your chickens a dry and airy house, and provide them with plenty of food and fresh water, then they are relatively easy to keep. The best advice, before you get your own chickens, is to talk to any friends and neighbours who keep chickens, visit your vet, talk to local 'chicken-fancier' groups, and generally do your homework until you know all the do's and don'ts of chicken-keeping.

How many eggs will you get?

Two healthy, well-looked-after chickens will give you anything from 6 to 14 eggs a week, all depending upon their breed, their age, the weather and the time of year. When everything is just right, a pair of hens will give you about 600 eggs a year – say 12 eggs a week. If the chickens get ill, or if you occasionally miss out on giving them their food and/or water, for whatever reason, then you can expect them to produce fewer eggs. Collecting and eating your first fresh egg will be an experience you'll never forget!

'Hey, look! The chickens have laid two eggs for our breakfast!'

OK...so who is the chicken now?

How to make a chicken house

Ask an adult to help

You need...

▷ A good supply of salvaged wood

▷ Handsaw

▷ Tape measure

▷ Try-square

▷ Cordless drill/driver and bits

▷ Hammer, nails, screws, string and fencing staples

▷ Six hinges and two bolts (locking mechanisms)

▷ Chicken wire

1 Our chicken house is 214 cm (84 in) long, 92 cm (36 in) wide and 122 cm (48 in) high and suitable for two chickens. It is made from odds and ends of salvaged wood. The construction and size of your chicken house will depend on how many chickens you have and the sizes of your bits of wood. The following steps give general information about our chicken house that you can use as a guide for building your own.

2 The nesting box part (see opposite) measures 76 cm (30 in) wide, 92 cm (36 in) deep and 61 cm (24 in) high with a similar size covered area below. Use a handsaw to cut the plywood or toungue-and-groove wood to size so that you have a roof panel at 92 cm x 76 cm (36 x 30 in), a base panel at 92 cm x 76 cm (36 x 30 in), a back panel 61 x 76 cm (24 x 30 in) and two side panels each at 92 x 61 cm (36 x 24 in). Join these panels to each other using battens and screws on the inside corners to make an open fronted box that stands on 61 cm (24 in)-long legs. Set the roof at a sloping angle by the addition of a plank of wood at the front about 15 cm (6 in) wide (see photograph opposite).

3 Clad the area under the nesting box with wood screwed to the legs but leave the side facing into the cage open.

4 Cover the triangular ventilation holes each side of the roof with chicken wire stapled in place.

5 Make a door to fit the front of the nesting box and fix it in place with two hinges and a bolt or catch.

6 Inside the nesting box is a horizontal stick, 23 cm (9 in) off the floor and 15 cm (6 in) from the back for the chickens to perch on and sleep at night. Fix this with screws.

7 Cut a door hole approximately 61 cm (24 in) high and 23 cm (9 in) wide in the side of the nesting box that faces into the cage. Cut a door to fit the doorway and hinge it at the bottom (so that when opened it forms a ramp).

8 To build the run use the battens to make 4 identical frames about 61 cm (24 in) wide and 122 cm (48 in) high. Join and reinforce the corners with little triangular blocks of wood and screws.

9 Take the four frames, screw them together in pairs, and fit them to the side of the nesting box.

10 Make a frame 122 cm (48 in) high and 92 cm (36 in) wide from battens, corner blocks and screws. Fix it to the end of the run with screws. For the door at the end of the run make another identical frame and fix it with hinges and a bolt or catch.

11 Cut a 3 ft batten and screw it inside the cage to make a horizontal support for the nesting box door to rest on when open. Now cut and fix a ramp to one side of the nesting box door, that runs from the horizontal support down to the end of the cage.

12 Cut, fit and staple chicken wire to the sides, top and door of the run. Add extra battens to reinforce the nesting box, run and doors wherever you think the structure needs to be strengthened. Screw or nail these in place.

13 Two horizontal sticks 229 cm (90 in) long reinforce the structure and form handles for dragging the house to new locations.

Make sure to bang *the* nail, not *your* nail – that would hurt quite a lot.

14 Attach string to the top of the nesting box door (inside the run) and run it through holes in and out of the nesting box so you can open and close the door from outside.

15 Spread wood shavings on the floor of the nesting box, provide food and water in the run and introduce your chickens to their new home.

How to cook eggs...

...boiled
Put two eggs in a saucepan, cover them with water and boil for five minutes. Carefully remove the eggs and slice their tops off with a knife. Use a spoon to eat the eggs, with some bread and butter.

...scrambled
Dribble a small dash of olive oil into a saucepan and put it on the heat. Whisk the eggs with a small amount of milk and pour into the pan. Keep stirring the egg with a fork until it's just cooked. Spoon the cooked egg out onto a slice of toast, sprinkle (if you like) with salt and black pepper, and eat straight away.

...poached
Put some water into a saucepan, pour in a splash of vinegar and put it on the heat. Break the eggs one at a time into the gently boiling water. Cook until the egg white goes solid. Spoon the eggs out, drain them carefully, place them on a slice of warm toast, and eat with your fingers. (If you like it, spread the toast first with some yeast extract.)

...fried
Dribble olive oil into a frying pan and heat it until it sizzles. Break the eggs one at a time into the pan. Leave the yolks whole or break them with a fish slice – the choice is yours. Use the slice to flip the egg over, wait until the edges are crisp and turn it out onto a fat slice of brown bread.

Wild berries

Which wild berries are safe to collect?

Be warned – some berries are poisonous! You *must* check with an adult before eating any wild berry. Blackberries are easy to identify and packed full of flavour. Eat them on their own or with sugar, or make them into a ice-slush drink, smoothie or milkshake.

What's so eco about wild berries?

Wild berries, such as black-berries and strawberries, are eco-stars on every count – they're completely organic, they're free if you take the trouble to go out and collect them, and they don't involve any packaging or transport to the shops.

Blackberries ↑

Where are the best berries?

The very best berries are always found out in the wilds, in quiet areas, away from roads, where not many people go. To put it another way, you don't want to be eating berries if there's a chance that they could have been blasted with polluting car-exhaust fumes, sprayed with weedkiller, sloshed with cowpats or dribbled with dog wee.

How to make a blackberry milkshake

You need...

▷ 3 handfuls of wild blackberries

▷ 2 large bowls

▷ Potato masher

▷ Open-textured cloth
(such as muslin)

▷ Wooden spoon

▷ Crushed ice

▷ Glass full of milk

1 Get all your blackberries checked over by a trusted adult – just to make sure you haven't picked anything that might be poisonous.

2 Remove anything that wriggles, squiggles, slithers or hops – things like flies, maggots, worms, caterpillars and bugs. Pick off any stalks or spiky bits, and throw away anything that looks dry, mouldy or in any way bad.

3 Wash the blackberries under running water, put them in one of the bowls (save a few for decorating) and squash them with the masher until they're nicely pulped.

4 Pour the pulp into the cloth over the other bowl. Gently press the pulp with the wooden spoon until all the juice and some of the thick bits have gone through the cloth into the bowl.

5 Add the milk to the berry juice, mix it together, put in the fridge untill it's cold, decorate with more berries and it's ready!

Butter

At school we were given a bottle of milk to drink during our break. Sometimes we would shake our bottles until the cream turned to butter! We would then give the warm and sticky left-over part of the milk to the school cat, and save the blob of butter to spread on our lunchtime sandwiches.

How to make butter

You need...

▷ Hand-sized jam-jar with screw-top lid

▷ Enough full-cream milk to fill the jar

▷ Fine-weave cotton cloth

▷ 2 Bowls

▷ Small pinch of salt

1 Sit in the sun with your screw-top jar full of rich, creamy milk and shake it up and down for about an hour, until the creamy part of the milk has formed into a little ball.

2 Unscrew the lid and use the cloth and one bowl to strain off the liquid (called 'whey'). Mix the salt into the butter in a separate bowl and put it in the fridge.

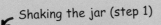
Shaking the jar (step 1)

Straining (step 2)

ECO TIPS

Crop dusting (spraying chemicals on plants)

Chemical farming and subsidies

Chemicals increase crop yields (meaning how much is produced), and government money in the form of farm subsidies keeps farmers happy, but both result in low-quality, low-priced food. Do you think this is a good idea?

'Milk quotas' and 'butter mountains'

Milk quotas – limits on how much milk each farmer could sell – were a government means of controlling milk production. This resulted in mountains of butter (made from the milk that couldn't be sold), imbalances in supply and costs, and low animal-welfare standards.

How does world trade affect you and the environment?

World trade affects everything from the environment and the well-being of farmers all over the world to your own health. Your liking for, say, lots of low-cost chocolate, and my liking for a cup of low-cost coffee, might mean that some poor farmers in somewhere like South America or Africa have to miss out on a square meal because they can't get a fair price for their produce. This may lead to lower-quality chocolate and coffee.

ECO ENERGY AND WATER

Wind turbine

Have you ever seen a wind turbine?

The biggest wind turbine in the world, built in Germany, is about 150 m (500 ft) high (20 times the height of a house), with a rotor-blade diameter of over 120 m (400 ft). The tip of the blade takes 5–8 seconds to travel a full circle. Giant turbines like these provide power for about 5,000 homes.

Engineers prepare to lift the blades of a huge turbine into position

Hundreds of turbines are placed together to make a 'wind farm'

What makes the wind blow?

If you open a window in your house in winter, you'll feel cold air rushing in. The same thing happens on a larger scale around our planet. The Earth's air or atmosphere is heated by the sun, but this doesn't happen evenly. Winds are created when areas of hot air (less dense) and cold air (more dense) move and mix in an effort to even out temperature differences.

↗ Wind pumps are used to pump water from underground

How does a wind turbine work?

Most wind turbines have anything from two to five blades, a bit like an old-fashioned aeroplane. Wind pushes on the blades, which forces them to move around. The spinning 'hub' in the centre then generates electricity.

What are the advantages of a wind turbine?

ADVANTAGES

* Wind is free
* Wind turbines don't produce CO_2 or radioactive waste like power stations do
* Wind turbines have a small 'physical footprint' (the amount of ground they take up) so the surrounding land can still be used for farming
* Small wind turbines can be erected at people's homes to generate off-grid energy (see page 15)

DISADVANTAGES

* Wind turbines only work when the wind blows!
* Some people think that wind turbines look ugly and are noisy
* Some people think that the whirling blades kill birds
* If it takes one giant turbine to power 5,000 homes, a city like London would need at least 6,000 turbines – but where could they be built?

Build a wind turbine!

Ask an adul
to help

You can build a wind turbine that will power a small
light for your den or shed. If your outdoor space is limited, make a
smaller version and consider fixing it to the top of the den or shed.
It's easy to make – just think about it as linking these five items
together:

✳ **Bicycle hub dynamo** – the bit that generates the power

✳ **Blades** – the bits that spin round in the wind, turning the hub

✳ **Mounting bracket and tail vane** – the bit that sits on the mast

✳ **Mast** – the bit that holds the blades, hub and tail up in the air

✳ **Solar LED shed light** – a bright, low-voltage light, connected
  to the hub by a cable

You need...

▷ DIY tools, including jigsaw,
  handsaw, cordless drill/driver and
  bits, and hammer

▷ 2 pieces of PVC pipe, 10 cm (4 in)
  in diameter and 60 cm (24 in) long

▷ Pair of compasses

▷ 2 pieces of exterior plywood
  about 30 cm (12 in) square

▷ Ruler and pencil

▷ 6V bicycle hub dynamo – we
  found ours on a rubbish tip but
  you can buy locally or online

▷ Screws, nuts, bolts, washers,
  plastic ties and jubilee clip (sizes
  to suit your found materials)

▷ U-shaped metal bracket for fixing
  the hub to the mast – ours came
  from an old gate

▷ Found item for the 'tail' – we used
  an old fish-barbecue grill and a
  sheet of plastic, but you could use
  an old tennis racket and the plastic

▷ 50 m (164 ft) 6V 2-core electric
  cable

▷ Electrical amalgamating tape

▷ 4.5 m (15 ft) long metal pipe for
  the mast – we used 2 old pieces
  joined together

▷ Rope and tensioning cleats

▷ 6V solar LED shed light kit

Wind turbine drawings

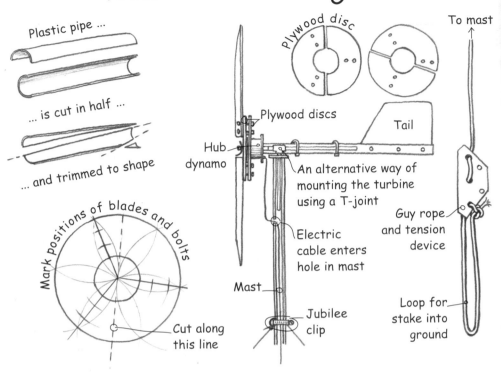

Plastic pipe ...

... is cut in half ...

... and trimmed to shape

Mark positions of blades and bolts

Cut along this line

Plywood disc

Plywood discs

Hub dynamo

Tail

To mast

An alternative way of mounting the turbine using a T-joint

Electric cable enters hole in mast

Mast

Jubilee clip

Guy rope and tension device

Loop for stake into ground

How to build the wind turbine

Making the blades (step 2)

1 Decide where you want the turbine to stand. It needs to be as near the light as possible and nowhere near overhead wires buildings or neighbours. Check with an adult before you start.

2 Saw each of the two pieces of pipe in half lengthways so that you finish up with four turbine blades (keep one for spare). Trim the blades to the finished shape (see drawing).

3 Use the compasses to mark two circles of plywood about three times larger in diameter than the hub dynamo. Cut out the discs.

4 On both discs, draw a circle in the centre that's the same size as the hub. Set the compasses to the radius of the plywood disc, spike the point anywhere on the circumference and draw an arc right through the circle. Reposition

Reinforce the discs with extra bolts (step 5)

the point of the compasses to where the arc intersects the circumference (you can use either intersection) and draw another arc as before. Repeat this procedure around the circumference until you have six 'petal' shapes (see drawing far left). Use a ruler and pencil to mark straight lines from the centre of the disc to the circumference through the centre of every other petal. Move the compasses point to the centre of the disc and mark bolt holes on the petal centre lines in roughly the positions indicated in the diagram (not critical). Mark a cut line between two petals. Then cut each disc in half and cut out the centre holes with a jigsaw (an adult will need to do this for you).

5 Fit the half-discs around the hub; ensure that the cut lines offset. Screw them to each other at regular intervals. Drill holes through the blades and plywood discs at the points already marked, and fix the blades in position using bolts, nuts and washers. Reinforce the discs with additional bolts as shown left.

Hub bracket, tail fixing and cable connection (steps 6–8)

Fitting to the mast (steps 9–10)

6 Bolt a U-shaped metal bracket to the back of the hub. Drill holes in the ends of the bracket that are large enough to take your mast (make it a loose fit so that the turbine can rotate as the wind changes direction). If you can't find a bracket, make one from scrap metal.

7 Fix the tail vane to the bracket by binding it with coat-hanger wire or clamping it with jubilee clips.

8 Connect the cable to the screws in the electrical contacts on the dynamo (fit one core to each contact) and bind with amalgamating tape. Ask an adult to help.

9 Fix the turbine on top of the mast using a washer and a jubilee clip above and below the U-shaped bracket. The fixing order is fit a jubilee clip about 15 cm (6 in) down the mast, slide a washer down the mast so it rests on the jubilee clip, slide the U-shaped bracket on the mast so it's resting on the washer, slide a washer so it rests on the top of the bracket and finish with a jubilee clip.

10 Dig a 30 cm (12 in) deep hole in the ground and put a brick or similar in the bottom of the hole for the mast to rest on. Tie four strong guy ropes to the mast and add tension devices as shown in the diagram on page 70.

11 Connect the electric cable to the solar LED light kit. If you like, you can run it down through the mast by making a hole at the top and another at the bottom. Then just wait for the wind to blow!

Photovoltaic cells

A photovoltaic (PV) cell, or solar panel, converts sunlight into electricity. It will make 'direct current' (DC) electricity, which is like that produced by a battery. Each PV cell contains a back contact, two silicon layers, an anti-reflective coating and a contact grid. A low-cost PV system is a great eco-friendly way to power small appliances.

Eco power

A really cheap PV cell will easily power a few LED lights, a mobile phone charger, a laptop computer, a small radio, a media player – in fact, almost any small electrical item that is normally powered by batteries. Just in case you or your parents are worried, a low-voltage item of this type is safe to handle. A solar-powered shed-lighting kit is a typical low-cost example, and is very easy to fit.

See if you can get the solar cell to light the bulb

Experiment and see what happens

Camp-fire circle

Ask an adult
to help

A camp-fire circle, which my grandfather used to describe as a 'cowboy camp fire', is an area where you can have a fire and do your cooking in relative safety. The circle is made up of a central pit (to contain the fire and stop it spreading), an inner ring of large stones and an outer raised ring of turf. The idea is that you sit on the raised ring with your feet braced against the stones. This way, you can cook without coming to any harm.

You need...

▷ Rope and 2 poles

▷ Bricks and large stones

▷ Garden tools

▷ Sledgehammer

1 Use a length of rope and two found poles, like our batten and iron rod, and mark or 'scribe' out a 305 cm (120 in) diameter circle. (The rope, when tied to the poles, should be half this length to create the right size of circle.)

2 Clear the turf with a garden spade and put it around the edge so as to make a raised ring or hump. Dig away a small bit for the entrance.

Mark out the circle and remove the turf (steps 1–2)

Digging an entrance (step 2)

74

3 Take earth from the centre of the ring and from other areas in the garden and use it to pad out the ring on both sides – so that you finish up with a big saucer shape.

4 Dig out a central pit, about 45 cm (18 in) deep and 60–90 cm (24–35 in) in diameter, and fill it up with bricks. Ask an adult to use a sledgehammer to break the bricks into small pieces.

↑ Place extra earth around the ring and smooth it out (step 3)

5 Use bricks to build little supports around the central pit, so that you have somewhere to rest cooking pans. Place the large stones around the edge of the pit.

Get toasting those marshmallows! ↘

ECO TIPS

What *is* the sun?

The sun is about 1.35 million km (840,000 miles) in diameter (100 times greater than that of the Earth), and made up mainly of hot gases. The temperature at its centre is at least 10 million degrees K (kelvin). The surface, however, is only 5,800 degrees K – say 20 times hotter than a cup of tea!

3D impression of a 'massively active' sun

How do PV cells work?

Things called 'photons' in sunlight are absorbed and passed through the material within the solar panel. The photons agitate particles called 'electrons' in this material, and the movement of these electrons creates electricity. To put it more simply, sunlight goes in one end and electricity comes out the other.

Different ways of using the sun's rays

* **Flat collectors** – an array of metal pipes or glass tubes through which water is passed. The sun shines on the tubes and heats the water. The resulting hot water goes to a storage tank.
* **Wide-angle collectors** – an array of metal tubes set together with a curved metal reflector. The curved metal concentrates the heat from the sun. These are also used to heat water.
* **Evacuated tubes** – an array of glass tubes that have mirror-like surfaces to concentrate the sun's rays. The sun heats a pointed copper lump that in turn heats water.
* **Trombe wall** – a hollow brick or concrete wall-like structure usually found in a conservatory. The sun heats the wall from the outside during the day, and the wall gives off heat to the inside during the night.

Solar tunnel

Be careful

A solar tunnel is like a one-man tent, but you grow plants in it. You can grow tomatoes or even orchids in the certain knowledge that they're going to be warm and protected from flies, birds, rabbits and other pests.

How to make a solar tunnel

You need...

- ▷ 5 battens; 3 at 180cm (70 in) long and 2 at 120 cm (47 in) long
- ▷ Handsaw
- ▷ Cordless drill/driver and bits
- ▷ Screws
- ▷ Blue plastic pipe; 2 pieces, 214 cm (84 in) long
- ▷ 4 wooden pegs
- ▷ Clear plastic film

Brace the tunnel at the top (step 3)

1 Screw four of the battens together to make a frame that's 180 cm (70 in) long and 120 cm (47 in) wide.

2 Reinforce the ends of the plastic pipe by banging wooden pegs into the ends. Screw through the tube ends and into the corners of the frame so you finish up with a tunnel shape.

3 Strengthen (brace) the tunnel with a batten fixed with screws that links the top curves.

4 Wrap the plastic film around the plastic tubes in one end of the tunnel and out the other until you have a complete tunnel. Seal the ends of the tunnel with short lengths of film (the film sticks to itself). Place your plants inside. Remove the tunnel for watering the plants.

Solar splash pool

Be careful

This paddling pool uses the power of the sun to heat up the water. Here you can make your very own 'concentrating solar thermal device' – this sounds fancy but just means something that creates heat by using the sun.

How does it work?

When the pool is full of cold water, you operate a hand pump to move some of the water up to the top of the slope. The water then dribbles out of holes in the pipe and falls onto a sun-baked corrugated-metal sheet. As it runs down the channels in this 'shute', the water heats up, and the pool is filled with warm water.

How to make the pool

You need...

▷ Plenty of straw, plus 2 extra bales

▷ Lots of rope and string

▷ Large plastic sheet 360 cm x 360 cm (142 in x 142 in)

▷ Sheet of corrugated metal, 240 cm (94 in) long and 90 cm (35 in) wide

▷ 7 wooden battens, 150 cm (59 in) long

▷ Offcuts of plastic guttering, 2 pieces at least 100 cm (40 in) long

▷ Hand pump – we used a wartime fire pump but you could use a low-cost bilge pump available from a chandlers

▷ 360 cm (142 in) length of hosepipe

▷ Old plastic water tank or some other container (optional)

▷ Household and garden tools such as tape measure, spirit level and handsaw

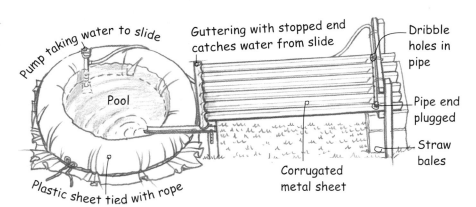

Pump taking water to slide

Guttering with stopped end catches water from slide

Dribble holes in pipe

Pool

Pipe end plugged

Straw bales

Corrugated metal sheet

Plastic sheet tied with rope

1 Decide on the size of your pool and form the straw into a sausage shape long enough to form the circumference. Bind the sausage up with rope or string so that you have a big fat hoop like a giant doughnut. Look at the drawings and see how the inner diameter and fatness of the hoop decide the size and depth of the pool.

2 Drape the plastic sheet over the sausage hoop and use a hose to fill the central space up slowly with water.

3 When the water starts to brim over, wrap the rope around the outside of the whole thing and knot it off securely.

4 Lay the corrugated sheet on the ground, and bang battens into the ground 15 cm (6 in) along from each corner. Saw off the tops of the battens so that the two nearest the pool are 61 cm (24 in) high and the

others are 120 cm (47 in). Link the shorter battens with a horizontal batten at the top, held in place with rope or string. Place two straw bales one on top of the other, between the other pair of battens. Add a horizontal batten on top of the bales and then another batten to the top ends of the vertical battens. Rest (not fix) the corrugated sheet on the battens. Add on guttering to the lower end of the corrugated sheet and another length linking the first piece of gutter to the pool.

5 Fit to your hand pump a hose that runs from the pool up to the top of the metal slope.

6 You now have a choice: either fix the top end of the hose to the top of the slope and make holes in the hose so that there is a well-placed dribble point above each of the channels in the corrugated sheet; or run the hose into a holding tank that, in turn, dribbles water through carefully placed holes.

Water-collecting

Be careful

In many countries, people take a bath or a shower every day, leave taps running and use automatic washing machines.

This means that we each get through around 30 buckets of water a day. Water is all around us, in lakes, rivers and the sea, but purifying and pumping it takes power (producing harmful carbon dioxide). Here is a way to collect and filter water and save on that power. The filtered water can be used for washing, washing-up or boiling (DO NOT drink it without boiling it first) and any waste water from the sink is drained into a bucket and used for watering plants.

How to make a water-collecting system

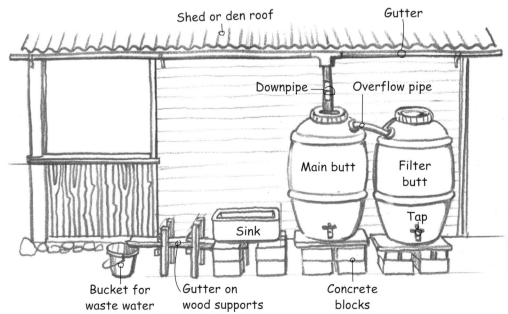

Shed or den roof

Gutter

Downpipe

Overflow pipe

Main butt

Filter butt

Tap

Sink

Bucket for waste water

Gutter on wood supports

Concrete blocks

You need...

▷ Six wheelbarrow loads of bricks and slabs

▷ Large sink

▷ 2 water butts with taps

▷ 100 cm (40 in) plastic pipe, 100 cm (40 in) guttering and tank connectors

▷ Drill with a bit of the same diameter as the plastic pipe

▷ 200 cm (79 in) long wooden batten

▷ Handsaw

▷ Tape measure

▷ Bucket

▷ 1 bag each of pea gravel, barbecue charcoal and sand

Cross-section of the filter system

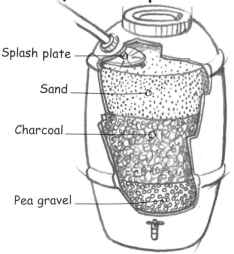

Splash plate

Sand

Charcoal

Pea gravel

1 Arrange the bricks and slabs so that you have platforms that can support the sink and the two water butts (one butt should be at a slightly higher level so that the water can run downhill from one to the other). The heights of the platforms should allow room for a bucket to sit below the tap in the filter butt, and for water to run from the sink along a gutter pipe into a waste bucket. Install the two butts and sink, and connect the main butt to the gutter with a downpipe.

2 Mark the position of the overflow pipe on the main butt and the inflow pipe on the filter butt. Drill holes and link the two butts with a short length of pipe.

3 Use odds and ends of batten and plastic guttering to make a channel running from the underside of the sink and down towards the waste bucket (which might need to be set in a hole in the ground).

4 Fill the filter butt with the layers of filter material – gravel, charcoal and sand – as shown in the diagram on the left.

5 If you like, you can paint the butts in your favourite colours to jazz them up a bit.

A hurricane is a mix of the worst rain and wind that you can ever imagine, and then some more

{ ECO TIPS }

Hurricanes and floods

According to the US government, human-caused global warming will result in longer droughts, heavier rainfall, worse floods, hotter heatwaves and bigger hurricanes. The report says that extreme weather events will be more commonplace and more intense. It's probably a good idea to talk about this with your teachers and parents to see what they think.

What is the Kyoto Protocol?

The Kyoto Protocol is a set of rules, decided by 137 countries, relating to discussions on climate change. The idea is that the rules will be used as a guide when the countries come to talk about such matters as greenhouse gas emissions. Although these countries have been talking since 1997, they haven't yet agreed on what they have agreed. How's that for complicated?

Weather station

This is a place where you can make observations about the weather and record your findings. It has various instruments and pieces of equipment that will help you monitor the weather and make your own forecasts or predictions.

Parts of a weather station

A weather station is made up of a **weatherproof box** (called a 'Stevenson Screen'), a **notebook** for keeping records, a 'minimum and maximum' **thermometer** to show the lowest and highest temperatures, a **barometer** to show air pressure, a **hygrometer** to show humidity (amount of moisture in the air), a **rain gauge** to show rainfall amounts, a **weather/wind vane** to show the wind direction, an **anemometer** to record the wind speed, and a **compass** so that you know which way the weather is moving.

Barometer

A barometer is an instrument used to measure atmospheric (air) pressure. High pressure indicates clear weather, and low pressure means clouds and rain. When you see your barometer readings going down as the air pressure falls, it's likely to rain; if they are going up, the sun will probably shine.

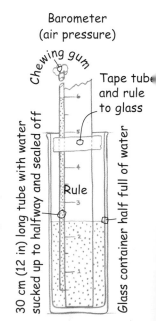

Barometer (air pressure)

Chewing gum

Tape tube and rule to glass

30 cm (12 in) long tube with water sucked up to halfway and sealed off

Rule

Glass container half full of water

84

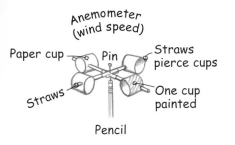

Anemometer
(wind speed)

Paper cup — Pin — Straws pierce cups
Straws — One cup painted
Pencil

Anemometer This is a windmill-like instrument that is used to indicate wind speed; the faster it spins the stronger the wind.

Hygrometer A hygrometer is used for measuring humidity, which is the amount of moisture present in the air. Daily hygrometer observations will enable you to record humidity patterns that will in turn help you to forecast the weather.

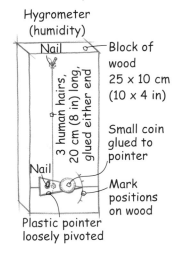

Hygrometer
(humidity)

Nail — Block of wood 25 x 10 cm (10 x 4 in)

3 human hairs, 20 cm (8 in) long, glued either end

Small coin glued to pointer

Nail

Mark positions on wood

Plastic pointer loosely pivoted

Rain gauge This is an instrument used for measuring rainfall. The diameter of the vessel or 'capture cup' and the scale that shows the depth of the captured water will enable you to measure how much rain has fallen over the last 24-hour period.

Weather/wind vane

A simple instrument that rotates with the wind and points to the wind direction (North, South, East or West).

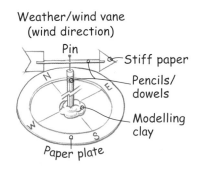

Weather/wind vane
(wind direction)

Pin
Stiff paper
Pencils/dowels
Modelling clay
Paper plate

Recording measurements
Every day at a regular time you need to record information as shown in the chart opposite.

Stevenson Screen
Designed by the father of Robert Louis Stevenson (the author who wrote *Treasure Island*), this is a cabinet for weather-recording instruments. The white, ventilated structure keeps the recording equipment both dry and shaded.

How to make a weather station cabinet

You need...

▷ 3 'louvred' cupboard doors about 61cm (24 in) high and 30 cm (12 in) wide

▷ Plywood offcuts for the base, back and roof (size to suit the louvered doors)

▷ 4 wooden battens, 180 cm (71 in) long plus a selection of offcuts

▷ Piece of cord about 61cm (24 in) long

▷ Hinges

▷ White paint

▷ Thin plastic sheet

▷ Hammer, handsaw, cordless drill/driver and scissors

1 Take two of the doors (one for each side of the cabinet) and screw a batten to each of the vertical edges.

2 Link the two sides with a base, back and roof made from plywood. Make sure there's a generous all-round overhang on the roof, with the highest end of the slope being at the front over the door. Use offcuts to strengthen the 'legs' as in the picture.

3 The front door of the cabinet is made from the third louvred door and is hinged at the bottom with a piece of cord attached like a castle drawbridge. When horizontal it is used for a surface to work on.

4 Paint the box white. Tack thin plastic sheet over the roof to keep the rain out, and put the instruments inside (apart from the rain gauge and wind vane, which need to be fixed on top).

Date	21/10
Time	10.20 am
Temperature	15°C/60°F
Barometric pressure	30.31
Humidity	High
Precipitation type and amount	Rain 6 mm (¼) in
Wind direction	NW
Wind speed	Low

ECO WHEELS

Eco bike

Your 'eco bike' can have whatever you want, but be sure to fit it with dynamo lights, a solar power pack and a trailer.

An eco bike is a means of transport that doesn't damage the environment. You could let your parents drive you all over the place in their car, but what's the point in wasting precious energy and smogging up the atmosphere when you can turn your wheels into a 21st-century, self-sufficient, energy-efficient, low-carbon, green machine? The humble bicycle has never been so cool!

The bike has been described as the most efficient machine ever invented ↘

Why is an eco bike 'low-carbon'?

Apart from the initial energy costs involved in the production of the bike, and in transporting it from wherever in the world it was made to a shop near you, your bike costs little or nothing to run. You don't need to buy any fuel and cycling doesn't produce polluting fumes. It's an altogether clean, carbon-mean machine.

Will it cost loads of money?

One visit to the local tip and talking with various family friends and neighbours provided us with a couple of bikes for spare parts, two dynamos, a solar power generator, and a whole heap of bits and pieces. There's a lot of interest these days in swapping bikes, bits of bikes, and all things bikey. This means that it needn't cost very much at all, even to get the bike itself in the first place.

How is it cool?

As a kid I had an old army bike. My sons were not so lucky (my youngest had to make do with a ladies' folding bike!). Nowadays, though, even cheap bikes are amazing, with front and rear suspension and at least ten gears. Look on the internet, or go down to your local bike shop, and see what eco additions you can stick on. How about a chopper bike with flashing solar lights, or a mountain bike with wind turbines on the handlebars for recharging your phone and media player? Why not customize a pedal go-kart for your younger brother or sister? Just use your imagination to invent stuff for your bike.

How to fit a dynamo to power the lights

1 The simplest option is to fit a 'rub-on-wheel' dynamo, as shown in the photograph on the right. So first get hold of one of these, and a pair of bicycle lights (one for the front and one for the back).

2 Study your dynamo, and the style and shape of your bike, and see how best it can be fitted on the front or back wheel without any danger of it getting in the way of the brakes, pedals and chain.

3 Clamp the dynamo to the frame so that when in the 'off' position it's clear of the tyre, and when in the 'on' position it's pressed hard against the tyre.

4 Fit the front and back lights to the bike.

5 With the frame acting as one 'wire', link the lights and the dynamo up with the other wire. Now when you turn the dynamo on and ride your bike the lights should work, powered by your legs!

It should press against the tyre, but only when in the 'on' position (step 3)

Dynamo plus battery

Some clever guys use a dynamo to charge a battery, which means you won't be without lights when you are stationary (this is a major drawback of dynamo lights). Look on the internet and see what you can find out about doing that.

Solar PV charger

A solar photovoltaic (PV) charger, as shown in the diagram below, is inexpensive to buy and will power all your mobile electronics – phone, music player, digital camera and so on. The charger converts and stores solar energy so that you can plug into it when one of your pieces of equipment needs topping up. When it comes to fitting it, think about how you use your bike and then attach the charger so that it can easily be removed. If you have brackets for it both at the front and back of the bike, you'll be able to move the charger to take advantage of the position of the sun.

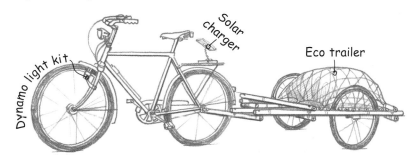

This bamboo trailer was designed by bike trailer company
Carry Freedom and made by students (see pages 94–95)

How to make an eco bike trailer

Be careful

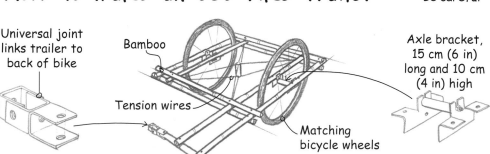

Universal joint
links trailer to
back of bike

Bamboo

Tension wires

Matching
bicycle wheels

Axle bracket,
15 cm (6 in)
long and 10 cm
(4 in) high

Now here's a good project for school

You need...

▷ 9 x 180 cm (71 in) lengths of 18 mm (¾ in) diameter bamboo, and/or lightweight metal tubing

▷ Tools such as tape measure, handsaw, hacksaw, hammer, drill, pliers and sandpaper

▷ Mild steel about 3 mm (⅛ in) thick for the two axle brackets and the universal joint

▷ Flexible metal cable – the sort that you can get from a chandlers (a shop that sells stuff for boats)

with 4 metal cable grips (to grip the return end of cable when forming a loop)

▷ Box, net, rack or seat

▷ 2 bicycle wheels of about the same diameter as the ones on your bike

▷ 50 bolts, 6 mm (¼ in) in diameter, 16.5 cm (6 ½ in) long, with washers and nuts to fit. These bolts are cut to length as required.

1 Have a look at the photographs opposite and below and the drawings on page 93, and collect together the material you are likely to use. The trailer is made from bamboo, old bike wheels and some bits and bobs that can be bought or made from scratch.

2 Carefully cut, drill and bolt together the nine lengths of bamboo that form the basic frame of the trailer. Sizes depend on how big or small you want the trailer to be, so you decide.

3 Make the axle brackets. Cut to size with a hacksaw, bend to shape with a hammer, drill holes as shown on page 93 and bolt them to the bamboo frame.

4 Make or buy the universal joint that links the trailer to the bike (see page 93). This is made from 3 identical piecs of metal 15 cm (6 in) long and 5 cm (2 in) wide, drilled and bent into U-shapes. Attach it to the trailer frame.

5 Fix metal cables across the diagonals of the frame using the cable grips at the ends and bolts through the frame.

6 Attach a box, net, rack or seat to the trailer, depending on what you are going to carry.

7 Fit the wheels, fix the universal joint to your bike's rear wheel spindle, and you're ready for an adventure.

Testing out the design in the school car park

Puncture repair

When I was a kid cycling to school with my friends, the country roads were so bad that we often got flat tyres. We were so well equipped and practised, though, that we flipped the bike over, repaired it and in ten minutes had it back on the road. Punctures are usually caused by nails, pins and thorns, and the repair is just a rubber patch stuck over the hole. You can make an inner tube last for many years, and that is the great thing about a bike generally – it's so easy and cheap to repair.

Can anyone mend a puncture?

You don't need to be strong, or have extra-big hands, massive thumbs or a huge brain – a simple puncture repair is one of those things that most kids can do.

Do you need loads of tools?

You need a puncture-repair kit, 2–3 tyre levers, a spanner to fit the wheel bolt, a small amount of water (from a tap, pond, puddle or even your own spit) and a bicycle pump. Don't try to do it too quickly until you understand the technique and how to use the rubber solution (the glue that sticks the patch on). If you rush, you'll risk nicking the inner tube with the tyre lever (another puncture to mend!) or wasting a patch if you don't get the preparation right.

How to mend a puncture

?

Always ask

1 Turn the bike upside down and use the spanner to remove the wheel or if space allows work with the wheel in place.

2 Slip the flat end of the tyre lever between the rim and the tyre and pull down until you can hook the end of the lever on a spoke. Repeat this with the other levers until one side of the tyre is free from the rim.

3 Pull out the inner tube, and remove whatever has caused the puncture.

4 Pump the tube up slightly, and listen, look and feel for escaping air. You might need to wet the tube, in which case you should look for bubbles rather than listen for air.

5 Once you have found and marked the hole, dry the tube, rub the area around the hole with sandpaper, and smear a large coin-sized blob of glue over and around the hole.

6 Wait until the glue has gone dull in appearance, then press the patch in place and leave it for about ten minutes.

7 Finally, push the inner tube back into the tyre, ease the tyre back onto the rim, refit the wheel, and pump up the tyre.

Punctures are easy to mend

After replacing a wheel, check the nuts are tight.

Bike adventure

Be careful

One summer, when I was about 11 years old, my grandpa and I decided to cycle about 25 miles to the nearest seaside.

It was great. We told gran where we were going, strapped a tent and our sleeping bags onto our bikes, and we were off. Of course, it was hard work – I was small and my grandpa was old - and we were both completely exhausted at the end of the journey, but it was a huge adventure!

How far in a day?

If you're keen and fit, you could walk about 16–19 km (10–12 miles) in a day, but give you a bike and, allowing for regular stops for food, rest and toilet breaks, you could easily cycle about 50–100 km (30–60) miles. Of course, these figures are only rough estimates, and a lot would depend on your bike, your age and your fitness, but the amazing thing is that a bike allows you to do all this distance with little or no extra effort. I think that cycling is much easier than walking – what do you think?

It takes planning!

* You must go with a loving and caring adult.
* Leave a detailed note describing your route and stop-off points.
* Take your mobile phone with you.
* It's more fun if you go in a group with brothers, sisters and/or friends.

* Make sure your bike is in good, safe condition – it should be well oiled, with good lights and brakes.
* Pack a puncture-repair outfit: puncture kit, tyre levers, spanner and pump (see pages 96–97).
* Take plenty of drinking water.
* Plan a route that uses small country roads and cycle routes, and avoid busy roads (you're not allowed on some big roads).
* Don't cycle after dark.
* Plan well ahead so that you have a good idea of how long it will take you to get to where you are going.
* Make sure you have adequate clothes for the likely weather.
* Make sure you have good maps.
* Cycle in single file and never leave any members of your group behind either when you move off after a stop or during the ride.

↓ A bike adventure can be amazingly good fun

ECO TIPS

Bikes for hire!

Get on your bike... or just hire one

It's not always easy to take a bike with you when you go on holiday or visit friends or family, but the good news is that most cities and big towns have created systems where you can hire a bike for the day. In one small town, there's a man who recycles old cycles. The idea is that a visitor buys one of his bikes at a giveaway price, uses it for a week or so, simply leaves it at the side of the road, and then gives the guy a ring to tell him where it is so that he can go and collect it and recycle it again.

Which is best in the city – a bike, a car or a tube train?

In most cities, it's much easier and quicker to cycle short distances than to spend ages stuck in a car in a traffic jam, or to buy a ticket, stand on a station platform, queue for a place in a hot, sweaty tube train, and then have to stand up for the whole journey if no seats are available.

Bike shortcuts and highway code

A bike adventure is good fun, but only if you stay safe and follow the local codes. Always be careful if you're racing through shortcuts that you aren't going to meet cars, trucks, trains or baby carriers coming the other way.

↑ The polluted skies over a road interchange in Bangkok in Thailand

Pollution from cars

✳ Cars produce toxic waste that damages our health.

✳ Road transport produces hydrocarbons, nitrogen dioxide, carbon monoxide, metals and a variety of organic compounds – all dangerous.

✳ Air pollution from transport produces acid rain, which damages crops, trees, our lungs and almost everything else.

Can we ever do without cars?

There's really no good reason why we can't figure out how to live without cars, or better still, invent a car that doesn't puff out huge amounts of poisonous emissions. This is what many people are trying to do (see the ideas described on page 109), but at the moment a 'green' car seems a long way off for most of us. Why not try thinking about how *you* would go about making the world a car-free place?

Cycling to school

Always ask

It's official – cycling is good for your brain! It will also improve your fitness.

Sometimes, though, it is just too far to cycle to school, or too dangerous (maybe because of the high number of parents driving their kids to school) – but what is too far or too dangerous? Anything over 8 km (5 miles) is probably too far, and the danger aspect is something you need to discuss with mum or dad.

Fun Cycling is healthy, good for the environment and low in cost, but above all it is just good fun. If you asked all your friends, family and neighbours what, when they were kids, was the one thing that really made a difference to their lives, most people would say that it was getting their first bike. Think about it – one moment you're limited to walking, going on a bus or being driven around in the family car, and the next you're whizzing off all over the place on your trusty bike.

Asthma If you're an asthma sufferer, you may wonder if cycling is a good idea, with all those hills and car fumes. Sadly, car fumes are bad for everyone's health, especially asthma sufferers, but you could use an anti-pollution mask while you're cycling. On the plus side, though, more bikes equal fewer harmful emissions, and doctors recommend moderate exercise for asthma sufferers as a way of building strength and fitness and helping their lungs.

Eco go-kart

A go-kart or 'soapbox cart' is, in its simplest form, a cart made from four wheels, a plank and a box or seat. If you think an eco go-kart (without an engine) is a bit boring, then think again. Building the kart is fun, and racing it downhill is even more exciting. When you get confident, maybe you could take part in an official race and even get a trophy! Then, if you want to try something a bit more advanced, you can have a go at racing a wind-powered 'land yacht' or 'kite buggy' (see the photo on the opposite page).

Are go-karts eco-friendly?

In the old days, people made and repaired just about everything – long before terms like 'eco' and 'recycling' were in common usage. With go-karts, the eco challenge is seeing if you can make one totally from recycled materials. If you succeed, it will give you so much more pleasure and enjoyment than if you just went out and bought one. Also, if it breaks down, you will know exactly how to repair it, since you were the one who made it in the first place!

Designing your kart

Your kart can be as big or small, as basic or fancy, as your materials and skills allow – and that's where the fun begins. If you go to an internet search engine and look up 'soapbox carts', you'll see that there are some miraculous designs out there. One person has made a cart entirely from old washing machines. If you're really interested, you could see if you could get your craft design and technology department at school involved, and set up a race.

How much will it cost?

Apart from the price of a few nuts and bolts, and the fuel costs involved in driving to collect bits and pieces from friends, family and the local tip, our kart (see page 107) cost almost nothing. The best thing to do is find the wheels first – after that you're cruising.

Karting rules

Keep off public roads is the main rule. The best place to use your kart is in your own garden or nearest park. For more variety, try private land with the owners' permission (they will tell you if it's safe) or on a beach. Also, think what may happen if the kart runs out of your control. Don't use it near pedestrians, obstacles or areas that may be dangerous. Also, never use the kart for stunts.

Go kiting and karting!
↓

How to build your own kart

Ask an adult
to help

You need...

▷ The whole point of this project is to use salvaged wood but here are some dimensions to use as a guide: one plank of wood or piece of plywood 92 cm (36 in) long, 46 cm (18 in) wide and 2.5 cm (1 in) thick plus 4 planks of wood 92 cm (36 in) long, 15 cm (6 in) wide and 1.8 cm (¾ in) thick.

▷ 2 metal 12 mm (½ in) 'threaded' rods, 100 cm (40 in) long with 8 washers and 4 nuts to fit.

▷ Large 13 cm (5 in) bolt, with a nut and 3 washers

▷ Child's car seat

▷ 2 small bike wheels

▷ 2 trolley wheels

▷ Rope, 200 cm (79 in) long

▷ Tools and materials such as cordless drill/driver and bits, handsaw, hammer, tape measure, nails, screws, bolts, washers and nuts

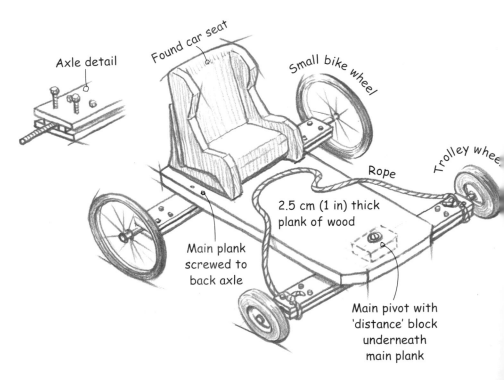

Axle detail

Found car seat

Small bike wheel

Rope

Trolley wheel

2.5 cm (1 in) thick plank of wood

Main plank screwed to back axle

Main pivot with 'distance' block underneath main plank

1 Sit down on the ground with your legs bent and braced – just as if you were sitting on a kart – and get a friend to measure the distance from the back of your seat to your feet. Allowing for a little extra at front and back, use a handsaw to cut the main plank to length.

2 Make the back axle by sandwiching one of the metal rods between two narrow planks. Then screw the whole thing to the main plank so that you finish up with a large T shape.

3 Make the front axle as you did the back one. Position it so that it crosses beneath the front end of the main plank. Use a block of waste wood as a distance piece sandwiched between the plank and the front axle (see diagram opposite). Then drill a large pivot hole through the centre of the plank, the block and the front axle.

4 With the main plank resting on the block and axle, pass the large bolt through the pivot hole, making sure you have one or more washers between the layers of wood. Then use two or more

nuts to fix the bolt so that it's secure but still allows the front axle to be turned.

5 Screw the seat firmly to the back end of the main plank.

6 Fit the four wheels onto the ends of the axles. Put washers each side of the wheels, fit the nuts and hammer over the ends of the axle rods (to stop the nuts from coming off).

This alternative design uses parts of a pram and old bits of wood

7 Drill two holes – one at each end of the front-axle planks – and use them to tie the steering rope firmly in place. Now all you need is someone to push you along!

A beautiful but deadly aircraft vapour trail

ECO TIPS

Flights that cost the earth

Why is it that most of the people who tell us that air travel is much cleaner than road transport – so clean that really it doesn't matter – are involved in some way with aircraft companies and travel organizations? Air travel is making our dirty air even dirtier. So it's a good idea to think about how we can still have great holidays without the need to fly.

Are holidays at home any good?

Just imagine swimming and snorkelling in the sea, pottering among rock pools, lying flat down in a field and looking up at the night sky, sleeping in a tent with a mate, picnicking, biking – holidays at home are only as good or as bad as you make them. OK, maybe you live in a city and you're short of cash, but what's to stop you and a group of friends from kitting yourselves out with tents and backpacks and going on a walking and camping holiday in the nearest bit of beautiful countryside? Talk to your friends, parents and teachers – they'll have plenty of ideas to inspire you. Do remember though, that if you go on a trip, you must go with a loving and caring adult.

Vegetable oil, hydrogen or poo – which does your car use?

Probably none of the above! No doubt your car, like most of them, runs on diesel or petrol (see page 101 for the facts about how much damage these cause). Yet, with any luck, we are just a step away from greener cars that will run on 'clean' forms of fuel such as vegetable oil or hydrogen. Many years ago, a chicken farmer called Harold Bate invented a car that would run on chicken manure, so anything's possible!

Strange but true – cars that produce nothing but water

Water is made up of two parts hydrogen and one part oxygen (that's what 'H2O' means), and we can use electricity to separate the hydrogen from the oxygen. If we reverse the procedure, we can get the electricity back – a bit like what happens on a space shuttle. So, if we were to use fuel cells that use hydrogen and oxygen to create electricity to run the engine, we could have electric cars that give off nothing more toxic than pure water as an emission.

Solar-powered buggy

Would you like to play with a solar-powered 'moon buggy'? You can buy all sorts of kits for making something along these lines, but our buggy is extra special on at least two counts: it can be made from easily found basic materials, and all the workings are on view. It's really simple – the top-mounted solar panel powers the motor, the motor drives the rear axle, and the rear axle turns the back wheels. Best of all, though, the design is flexible enough to allow for a whole range of modifications.

A cute little solar buggy – note the huge photovoltaic (PV) panel

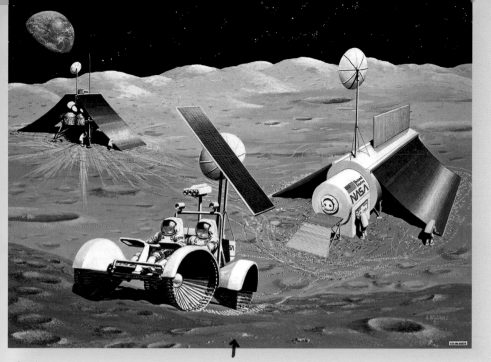

'Solar Power for Lunar Living' – this is a 'concept' drawing showing how solar panels might be used to power a camp and a buggy on the moon's surface

Looks complex but it's really simple

The good eco bit about this machine is that almost everything on it can be made either from things like plastic cotton reels, foam tubes and cardboard or from items scavenged from other toys. You have two options: you can settle for building the basic form and leave it at that, or you can build the basic form and then make modifications. For example, you could dramatically increase the size of the solar panel and motor and make a larger vehicle, you could have a motor for each wheel, you could design a much fancier body, you could use the model as a prototype for a large go-kart-type buggy that a person could actually sit on – there are lots of exciting possibilities, so let your imagination run wild.

How to make a solar-powered buggy

You need...

▷ About 75 cm (30 in) of 9 mm (⅜ in) square-section wood

▷ Handsaw

▷ Household items such as scraps of wood, stiff cardboard, masking tape, PVA glue, battery-type cables and switches, hole punch, scissors and a strong elastic band

▷ 2 x 20 cm (8 in) lengths of 4.5 mm (³⁄₁₆ in) diameter wooden dowel

▷ 4 cotton reels and 1 slightly smaller cotton reel

▷ About 15 cm (6 in) of foam tubing, large enough to be a tight sleeve-like fit on the cotton reels

▷ Plastic 'sleeve'

▷ Small, low-voltage, battery-driven, model makers' motor

▷ Photovoltaic solar panel – large enough to drive the motor

1 Have a scavenge to see what you can come up with. Things like the cotton reels are common enough, so it's only when you come to the electrics that you might have difficulties. Items like the motor and the fine wire cables can usually be found on and in broken torches, radios and remote-controlled cars.

2 When you've found all the bits, start by cutting the 75 cm (30 in) section of wood into four lengths using a handsaw – you need two about 23 cm (9 in) long and two about 13 cm (5 in) long.

3 Glue the wood together so that you have a chassis frame about 25 cm (10 in) long and 13 cm (5 in) wide. Strengthen the corners of the frame with small triangles of stiff card.

4 Cut out four more little triangle shapes for the axle supports, punch holes to take the axles, and be ready to stick them in place on either side of the chassis frame.

5 Stick the two front axle supports to the chassis, run the front dowel through its axle supports, bind the ends with the masking tape – until they are a nice tight push-fit for the cotton reels – and then push the cotton reels into place.

6 For the back axle, repeat the masking tape binding bit as in step 5, only this time you need to have three bindings, one each for the road

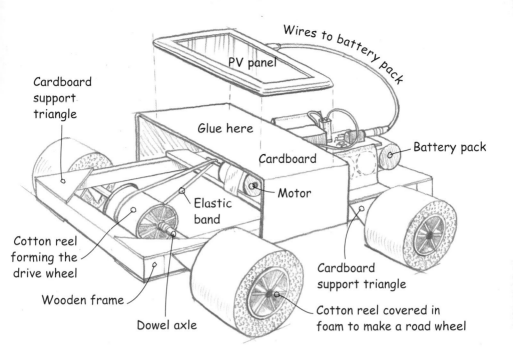

Cardboard support triangle

PV panel

Wires to battery pack

Glue here

Cardboard

Battery pack

Motor

Elastic band

Cotton reel forming the drive wheel

Wooden frame

Dowel axle

Cardboard support triangle

Cotton reel covered in foam to make a road wheel

wheels and one for the drive wheel
in the centre. Fit the drive wheel,
position the elastic band as shown,
stick on the axle support triangles,
and then fit the two road wheels.

7 Cut the foam tubing to make
tyres and slide them in place
over the cotton-reel wheels.

8 Cut, fit and glue the motor
mounting board in place
across the chassis.

9 Fit a found plastic sleeve on
the shaft of the motor, cut
a V-slot in the sleeve (for the
elastic band), and use the masking
tape to strap the motor to the
mounting board.

10 Cut a length of cardboard
to support the PV panel and
glue the ends to the sides of the
chassis so that the solar panel is
looking to the sky. Glue the solar
panel onto the cardboard.

11 Fit the cables to the solar
panel and the motor, stand
the buggy in the sun, and just see
what happens (it will move by
itself but you cannot steer it).

12 Finally, when everything is
up and running and you have
made any necessary adjustments
to the basic machine, you can start
thinking about how you're going to
decorate your buggy.

ECO GIFTS

Eco bling

Bling, if you didn't know already, is big, bold, expensive, sparkly jewellery, the sort made famous by hip-hop artists.

Previously, the word 'bling' described the star-like flash of light that we see in cartoons and adverts when someone smiles. So, if the bursts of light from flashing jewellery and cartoon smiles could make a sound, then they would go 'Bling!'. Eco bling is the same type of jewellery, but made cheaply from recycled waste materials.

→ Eco bling can be as big, bold and cool as you want to make it

Why eco bling is a good gift idea

Firstly, you're not trashing the environment even more by wasting money on a useless gift. Secondly, you're rescuing and recycling things that might otherwise be thrown away. Lastly, because you're custom-building the bling, you can tailor it to suit someone's style.

What can you use?

You can make eco bling from just about any stuff that comes your way – old coins, bits of broken watches and clocks, bottle caps,

116

electronic components, cogs from old engines, cleaned-up spark plugs, bits from an old socket spanner set…anything you like the look of and is OK for you to use. Always check with an adult first in case something is too valuable, sharp, pointed or toxic to be suitable. Never use anything that could cause an injury.

Making some heavy bling

I chose to make this example of an eco bling bracelet from a collection of key rings, marine chain shackles and swivels, metal washers, and coins with holes in the centre, for six good reasons. I like the feel of high-quality metal components (the sort of thing you would see in a chandlers and/or in engineers' workshops),

I have always collected such items, I like the weight, they won't rust or tarnish, they can be put together in various ways, and they can be swiftly taken apart and reused when I want to go on to other things.

Button wristlet

Long ago, when Europeans first settled in America, their everyday items were of great interest to the native American peoples, because they were so different to their own hand-crafted items. American native and cowboy costumes of the late 19th century often included highly decorative wristlets, bangles and necklaces made from these everyday items, such as coins, mirrors, glass beads, copper wire, buttons and brightly coloured fabrics.

Buttons are eco gems

When my great grandmother died, my grandmother inherited her button box, and then when she died my mum inherited her buttons. Buttons are great examples of good eco recycling, in that they are used and reused over many generations. Old buttons are also part of our historical heritage – I have some brass buttons that my grandfather wore on his uniform when he was a fireman in London during the wartime 'Blitz' in the early 1940s, and a button that my great grandfather carved from a piece of whalebone.

Where can you get buttons from?

Start by asking all your relations and friends, and then look around car-boot or garage sales, jumble sales and flea markets. Don't forget that some buttons are valuable. For example, one of the pearl-like buttons we used in our wristlet is in fact a real pearl from a hat pin, the sort of thing ladies wore every day a few generations ago.

Making a native American button wristlet

A quick look on the internet at pictures of native American costumes will show you that buttons were used in much the same way as beads. They were threaded onto cords and/or bone pins and rods to make both curved and straight jewellery – things like bangles, headdress bands and belts. Start by sorting your buttons into similar types – same colour, same shape, same material – and then simply experiment by putting them on two strands of strong thread or elastic until you're happy with the result.

You need...

▷ Two large needles

▷ Strong thread

▷ Buttons

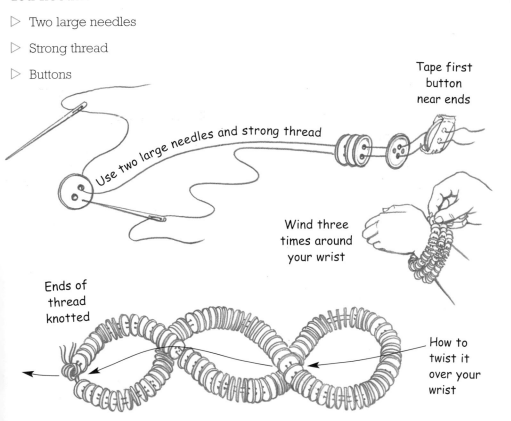

Use two large needles and strong thread

Tape first button near ends

Wind three times around your wrist

Ends of thread knotted

How to twist it over your wrist

119

Felt shoulder bag

? Always ask

Felt is a type of cloth that is made by mashing and squeezing bits of woolly fleece until it matts together. The wool could come from a sheep, a goat, a llama or even a yak. Almost all other fabrics are woven or knitted, but if you could travel back in time 6,000 years to Turkey you would find that felt was all they used. Nomadic Mongolians nowadays use felt for clothes, shoes, hats and yurts (their houses). The green material on billiard, pool and card tables is made from felt. Cowboy hats were also made out of felt.

Eco fabric
Felt is very eco-friendly. It more or less lasts for ever, it's made from natural materials and it has unique insulating qualities. You can make it from old woollen blankets, sweaters and scarves – perhaps even that horrible sweater your aunt knitted for you (you know you can't throw it away, but maybe it could shrink in the wash and then get recycled…).

How to make a felt bag

If you were to put your favourite super-smooth 100% wool sweater in the washing machine and run a high-temperature programme by mistake, the item would shrink to about half the size, the texture would be thick and lumpy, the colours would run and blur, it would be super-strong – and you would be very upset! The good news is that you can use this 'felting' effect to create a really cool bag. We got the idea for this design from a native American bag – the sort that a warrior wore on his back. If that's too macho, and you'd prefer it to be more pink and sparkly or catwalk chic, then just get your pens out and design your own eco bag. If bags aren't your thing, I am sure someone you know needs a bag-for-life for their weekly shopping – imagine how impressed they will be! Before you start, though, make sure that the woollen items you intend to use are not precious to someone.

You need...

▷ A single-bed-sized 100% wool blanket (we got ours from a charity shop) and a brightly coloured, knitted 100% wool sweater for pockets or decoration

▷ Thin or tracing paper

▷ Brightly coloured woollen yarn to complement the colours of the sweater and/or blanket

▷ Household items such as scissors, tape measure, buttons, chalk, hole punch, pins, needles, sewing cotton and large darning needle

These lovely bright colours are perfect 🡵

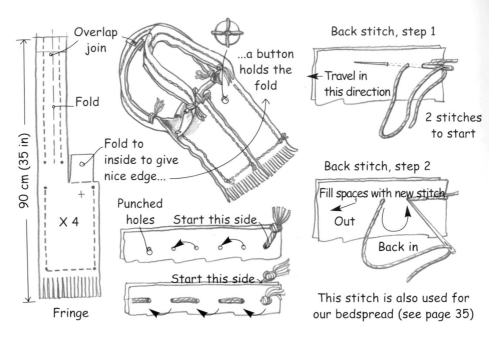

Overlap join

Fold

90 cm (35 in)

X 4

Fringe

Fold to inside to give nice edge...

Punched holes

...a button holds the fold

Start this side

Start this side

Back stitch, step 1

Travel in this direction

2 stitches to start

Back stitch, step 2

Fill spaces with new stitch

Out

Back in

This stitch is also used for our bedspread (see page 35)

1 Put your old 100% wool item in the washing machine, add powder or liquid and wash on the hottest setting. It will shrink to about half to one-third of its original size. A blanket will make a big bag and a jumper a small one.

2 Choose a scale (size) that allows you to get four identical pieces from your fabric using the pattern above. Transfer the pattern to thin paper, trim it to shape, pin it onto the shrunken fabric and cut it out. Repeat until you have four identical shapes.

3 'Tack' these identical shapes together (using big temporary stitches) and use coloured chalk to

mark in the position of the final stitch holes, about 2.5 cm (1 in) apart. Use a hole punch to make holes for these stitches.

4 Double up the woollen yarn twice so that it is four strands thick, and sew the felt cut-outs together with large, in-and-out stitches. Work right around in one direction, and when you get to the starting point change direction – so that you fill in the blanks on the return run. Or use back stitch as shown.

5 Finally, remove the tacking stitches, add pockets and decoration. Fold the edge flaps as shown in the diagram and photo and hold them in place with a button.

ECO TIPS

What happens to all the waste?

In the developed world, we each throw out our own bodyweight in rubbish every 6–7 weeks. We do recycle things like glass and metal, but for the most part we either bury or burn our rubbish. The buried stuff oozes out poisons for several lifetimes afterwards, while the burnt stuff fills the air we breathe with huge amounts of toxic fumes.

Should we buy less?

One look around a car-boot or garage sale shows that the world is sinking in a sea of rubbish – plastic toys, mobile phones, old clothes and so on. The more we have, the more we want, and we always want the latest model, discarding the previous one even if it's not broken. So the answer is yes!

Traditional landfill site

Postage-stamp bowl

Always ask

'Philately decoupage' is the fancy name for this technique, but it only means decorating things with postage stamps!

'Philately' is the study and collection of postage stamps, and 'decoupage' is the craft of decorating objects with paper cut-outs.

Eco decoupage

Decoupage has always been eco-friendly, simply because the craft uses saved paper (in this case postage stamps) to create decorative items. If you don't think that postage stamps are very exciting, there's no reason why you can't use pictures printed out from your computer, bubble-gum wrappers, fruit wrappers or labels from your favourite food instead – in fact, you can use anything as long as it's made of printed paper. Remember that some postage stamps are worth huge amounts of money, so it would be better not to use those for this project!

What can you cover with decoupage?

You can decorate just about anything that has a firm and permanent surface. Small items, such as a box, bowl, dish, book or picture, are a good starting point, and for a more ambitious project try a chair, side table or mirror. Decoupage screens are also good.

← The perfect present for a stamp collector!

You need...

▷ Plastic or wooden bowl

▷ Sandpaper

▷ Stamps

▷ Water in a spray container

▷ PVA glue

▷ 1–4 cm (½–1½ in) paintbrush

▷ Water-based high-shine varnish

1 Take a found plastic or wooden bowl and use a piece of sandpaper to rub it down to a slightly matt (roughened) finish.

2 Spray your postage stamps with water to make them thoroughly damp.

3 Give the whole bowl, inside and out, a coat of PVA glue – the sort of glue that you use to stick wood, paper and fabric.

4 Take your dampened stamps and use the PVA glue to stick them one at a time to the bowl. Make sure that the stamps are pressed firmly down, with no raised corners or air bubbles.

5 Continue until every part of the bowl has been covered.

6 Finally, when the whole thing is completely dry, give it several coats of high-shine varnish and the task is finished.

Furoshiki wrap

In Japan, a 'furoshiki' is a piece of pretty cloth used to carry just about anything.

Items that can be carried this way include books, bottles, fruit, documents, clothes, groceries and gifts. The size, shape and design of the cloth, and the way the furoshiki is wrapped and knotted, are all very important. So, for example, a large furoshiki wrap that is used for carrying heavy groceries might be made of stout cotton and knotted so that there are two carrying handles, whereas a

Furoshiki-wrapped gifts ↘

Knotting the furoshiki

fragile present might simply be wrapped in a delicately printed silk. The wonderful thing about a gift that is wrapped in a furoshiki is that the wrapping is considered to be just as important as the gift, and it is reusable.

The quality, texture and knotting techniques of the furoshiki are first admired, the gift is then unwrapped, and finally the furoshiki cloth is carefully folded and either reused for another gift or employed as a scarf, tablecloth or whatever might be appropriate.

Meaning

Furoshiki comes from two words – 'furo', meaning bath, and 'shiki', meaning spread. The complete word was first used in Japan during a time called the 'Edo period' when people going to public baths wrapped up their clothes in a special cloth.

How to use furoshiki wrap

Next time you're buying a present for your grandmother, you could get her a box of chocolates and a silk headscarf, and carefully wrap the chocolate box up in the headscarf. Or, if you study the diagrams on the next two pages, you'll see that there are furoshiki wrapping solutions for just about everything, whatever its shape or size.

Furoshiki examples

Square present, step 1

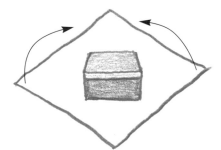

Round present, step 1

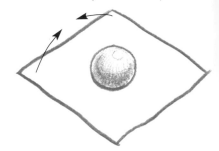

Square present, step 2

Tie opposite corners

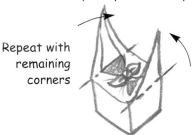

Round present, step 2

Tie corners together to form loops

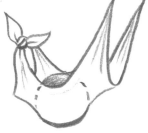

Square present, step 3

Repeat with remaining corners

Round present, step 3

Pass one loop through the other to make a carry handle

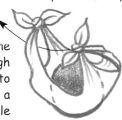

The knot: pass corners around each other...

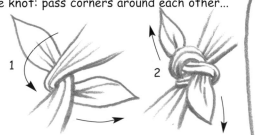

...then back through, and pull tight

Round present, step 4

Two books, step 1

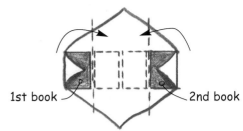

1st book — 2nd book

Long present, step 1

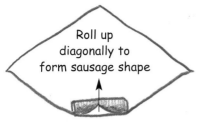

Roll up diagonally to form sausage shape

Two books, step 2

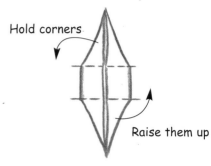

Hold corners

Raise them up

Long present, step 2

Fold up the two ends

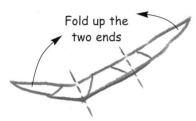

Long present, step 3

Pass the ends around each other...

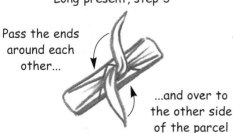

...and over to the other side of the parcel

Two books, step 3

Twist the ends around...

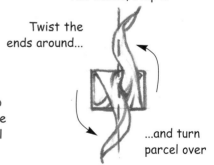

...and turn parcel over

Long present, step 4

Turn it over and tie the ends

Two books, step 4

Twist and tie to form handles

Books hang downwards

Patchwork rag bag

Always ask

Most of us have seen old patchwork quilts and cushions made out of hundreds of little hexagonal scraps of fabric. These scraps were all sewn together with incredibly small hand stitches, and the results are quite amazing. Patchwork using rags, however, is quite different. The patchwork is made from torn strips of fabric, with the torn edges fully on view, and the whole thing is put together on a sewing machine, which saves a lot of time.

Eco patchwork

We own a piece of patchwork, made over 100 years ago by an ancestor of ours, that uses all sorts of bits from worn-out clothes. Finding a new life for old clothes is even better than putting them in the recycle bin.

How to make the rag bag

You need...

Finished bag

▷ A selection of fabrics

▷ Backing fabric that is twice the size of the bag that you want to make

▷ 2 lengths of strong braid or belt material for the handle straps

▷ Sewing machine

▷ Household items such as scissors, tape measure, chalk, pins, needles and sewing cotton

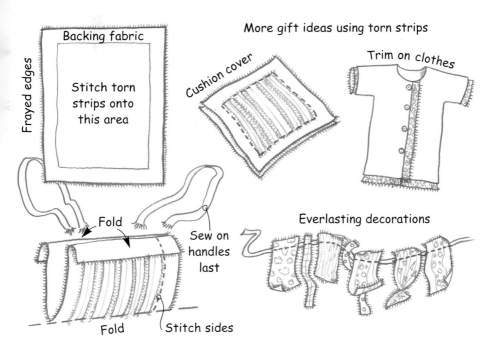

Backing fabric

Stitch torn strips onto this area

Frayed edges

More gift ideas using torn strips

Cushion cover

Trim on clothes

Fold

Sew on handles last

Everlasting decorations

Fold

Fold

Stitch sides

1 Tear your chosen fabric into about 34 strips, each about 90 cm (35 in) long and 5 cm (2 in) wide. Don't worry about the frayed edges, or if the strips vary in width along their length.

2 Set the sewing machine to zigzag, and stitch the strips onto a piece of backing fabric that is about 50 cm (20 in) wide and 90 cm (35 in) long – this will make a bag 50 cm (20 in) wide and 40–45 cm (16–18 in) deep. Here the strips are running down the length of the fabric, but there's no reason why you can't go for another direction or have overlapping strips.

3 Fold the ends of the backing fabric over so that the ends of the torn strips are covered up, and fix the folded flaps in place with zigzag stitches.

4 Fold the whole thing in half so that you have the bag shape, and fix the shape by running a line of zigzag stitches about 2.5 cm (1 in) in from the edges of the sides.

5 Take two lengths of strap for the handles, pin them in place at either side edge of the bag, and fix them in place with a rectangular shape of zigzag stitches. Use cotton of a contrasting colour for a bold effect.

131

ECO BITS AND PIECES

Dirty eco facts

* If every person on planet Earth throws away about 1 kg (2 lb) of rubbish every day, and there are 6,000 million people in the world – these figures allow for people who throw away a lot less or a lot more – then the total is 6,000 million kg (12,000 million lb) of rubbish every single day. **How dirty can you get?**

* If some plastics – like an old CD that you threw away the other day – take about 500 years to break down in landfill sites, it could be that your CD will be discovered in an archaeological dig in, say, the year 2500. **What will future people think of us?**

* If you use about 225 litres (about 50 gallons) of water for a 10-minute shower, and you live for 80 years, then 225 x 365 = 82,125 litres (50 x 365 = 18,250 gallons) in a year x 80 = about 6.5 million litres (about 1.5 million gallons) in your lifetime! **Is it time to start taking fewer, shorter showers?**

* The world's population is growing fast – in the year 1800 it was about 900 million, in 1900 it was about 1,600 million, in 2000 it was about 6,000 million, and it's still rising. **How many people do you think there'll be in the year 2100?**

✳ Half the people in the world are unhappy and unwell because they eat too much and are too fat, while the other half are unhappy and unwell because they eat too little and are too thin. **What is the reason for this?**

✳ When farmers poison bugs (things like greenfly), they're poisoning and/or starving other creatures that feed on the greenfly. If we poison greenfly at one end of the line, we'll be damaging creatures like ants, birds and ourselves at the other. **Is there perhaps another way of controlling bugs?**

✳ Livestock, meaning animals like sheep and cows, fart so much that they produce more greenhouse gas than cars. The global consumption of meat is going up rather than down. **Should people eat less meat?**

✳ A ceramic coffee or tea mug will last for hundreds of years, while foam and plastic cups are used once and instantly thrown away. We threw away 25 billion foam cups in 2007. **Why can't we go back to using ceramic mugs?**

✳ Every tonne of recycled paper saves 17 trees from being cut down. The USA cuts down 68 million trees a year to make about 65 billion pieces of junk mail. **Why don't we use more recycled paper and say no to junk mail?**

Eco gadgets

There are some amazing energy-saving eco gadgets around. They range from wind-up radios, solar-powered radios, torches and mobile chargers to wind-powered lights and toys powered by wind and sun. The photographs on these pages will give you some idea of the variety of eco gadgets that's available for you to choose from.

Photovoltaic charger for batteries and mobile phones

Wind-up torch

Solar powered multicoloured lighthouse

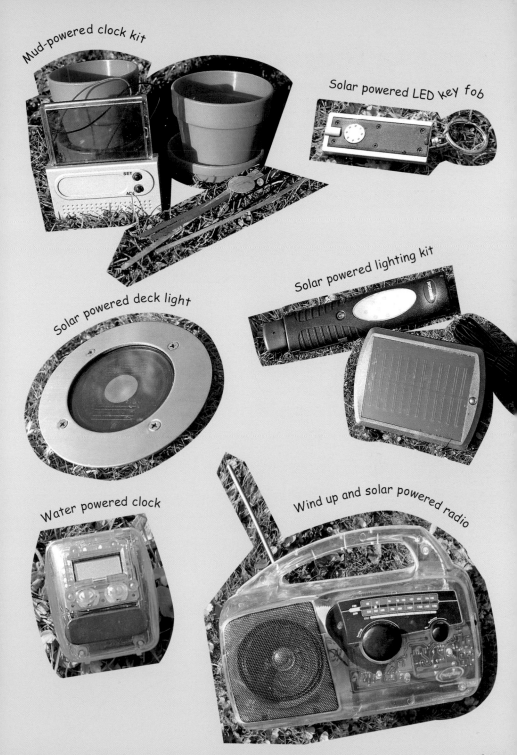

Mud-powered clock kit

Solar powered LED key fob

Solar powered deck light

Solar powered lighting kit

Water powered clock

Wind up and solar powered radio

Websites

Most eco websites are a well-balanced mix of fun and facts. Be aware, though, that some are no more than greedy people dressed up in 'eco-green clothes' who are only really interested in getting hold of your money. If you don't like the way that a website seems to be pushing, bullying or even shaming you into buying a product or making a donation, then switch off. Never give out any personal details.

* ECO NEWS – energy facts for teenagers, from Wellington in New Zealand – www.wcl.govt.nz/teens/eco_news.html

* ENVIROLINK – environmental information – www.envirolink.org

* GREEN GUIDE – run by the National Geographic Society – www.thegreenguide.com

* HEARTS AND MINDS – environmental fun for kids – www.heartsandminds.org

* KIDS ONLINE RESOURCES – click on 'science' and 'ecology' – www.kidsolr.com

* KIDS FOR A CLEAN ENVIRONMENT (Kids F.A.C.E.) – environmental issues for children – www.kidsface.org

* PLANETPALS – ecological fast facts for kids – www.planetpals.com

* ENVIRONMENTAL KIDS CLUB – run by the US Environmental Protection Agency – www.epa.gov/kids

* RODALE INSTITUTE – organic solutions – www.rodaleinstitute.org

* PERSONALLY GREEN – making individual eco changes – www.personallygreen.com

* ECOKIDS – Canada's environmental destination for kids – www.ecokidsonline.com

* KIDS PLANET – all about wildlife – www.kidsplanet.org

* GLOBAL WARMING – all about global warming – www.epa.gov/globalwarming/kids

* NC4K! – nature challenge for kids with activities and games – www.davidsuzuki.org/kids

* SELF-SUFFICIENCY – www.self-sufficient.co.uk

Eco glossary

* AIR POLLUTION – Presence of poisonous substances in the air that cause harmful environmental effects.

* ALTERNATIVE ENERGY – Energy derived from a source other than fossil fuels, such as wind or sun. An 'alternative energy home' is an off-grid home that uses non-fossil energy such as wind and solar power.

* BIODEGRADABLE – Describes something like cardboard that is capable of breaking itself down by biological means into basic natural materials, and therefore doesn't harm the environment.

* CARBON DIOXIDE (CO_2) – Greenhouse gas produced by burning wood and fossil fuels.

* CARBON EMISSIONS – Fumes released into the atmosphere that increase carbon dioxide and other greenhouse gases.

* CARBON FOOTPRINT – Measurement (in units of carbon dioxide) of the impact human activities have on the environment in terms of the amount of greenhouse gases generated.

* CLIMATE CHANGE – Name that's often used to describe the effects on the world's climate of global warming.

* COMPOST – Rotted organic waste; things like food and paper that decompose naturally and can be used to enrich the soil.

* CONSERVATION – Preserving and renewing both human and natural resources.

* CONTAMINANT - Physical, chemical, biological or radiological substance that poisons air, water or soil.

* EARTHSHIP – Term used to describe a self-sufficient home.

* ECO-FRIENDLY – Describes something that is not harmful to the environment.

* ECO-GREEN – Another term for 'eco-friendly' or 'green'.

* ECOLOGY – Study of the relationship between living organisms and their environment; the way that humans, plants, animals interact with the Earth all around them.

✳ ECOSYSTEM – The way that animals, plants, fungi and micro-organisms live and relate one to another in a particular area.

✳ ECO-WARRIOR – Certain type of environmental activist, often depicted in the media as a long-haired 'hippy'.

✳ EMISSION – Release of gases, liquids and/or solids from a process such as driving a car.

✳ ENVIRONMENTAL IMPACT – Any change to the environment that is the result of human and/or natural activity.

✳ FOSSIL FUELS – Remains of plant and animal life that have become fossilized into substances such as coal, oil and natural gas, which we currently use a lot of to provide us with energy. Burning fossil fuels harms the planet.

✳ GLOBAL WARMING – Heating-up of the whole planet caused by 'greenhouse' gases getting trapped in the lower atmosphere (see also Greenhouse Effect).

✳ GREEN – Often used to describe eco-friendly people, systems, groups and ideas.

✳ GREENHOUSE EFFECT – Warming of the Earth's surface and lower atmosphere (see also Global Warming).

✳ GREENHOUSE GASES – These include carbon dioxide, methane and ozone, which are involved in global warming.

✳ LANDFILL - Hole in the ground where we dump and then bury solid waste that takes ages to break down.

✳ NON-RENEWABLE ENERGY – Limited, one-off supply of energy that we get from fossil fuels such as oil, gas and coal.

✳ OFF-GRID – Not part of the normal system of supplying water, gas, oil and electricity.

✳ OZONE HOLE – Hole in the protective layer of the gas ozone, as seen over the Antarctic and Arctic regions, part of Canada, and the north-eastern United States.

✳ PASSIVE HOME – Home that uses natural things such as hot air that rises, black surfaces that absorb heat and white surfaces that reflect heat to create pleasant, eco-friendly living conditions.

Eco action plan

Why not discuss your ideas to help the environment with your family and friends? This page lists some things you can take action on immediately, and gives some suggestions for organizations you may like to contact. Imagine what you would like to do in the future to help the environment. Think about the impact your life is going to have on the world around you, and how you might improve things.

Immediate action

- ☐ Use only energy-saving lightbulbs, and turn off lights when not needed

- ☐ Use your bike (when it's safe) or public transport

- ☐ Use the car much less

- ☐ Avoid packaged food

- ☐ Don't eat battery chicken

- ☐ Don't nag your parents about getting new clothes

- ☐ Wear warmer clothes in winter to save heating

- ☐ Turn down the heating

- ☐ Turn off all stand-by equipment at night

Relevant organizations

You MUST ask your parents' advice and permission before joining or contacting any organization, as only they will know if it's safe or appropriate for you.

- ☐ Greenpeace

- ☐ World Wide Fund for Nature (WWF)

- ☐ Save the Children

- ☐ The Green Organisation

- ☐ Centre For Alternative Technology (CAT)

- ☐ Selfsufficientish

- ☐ Voluntary Service Overseas (VSO)

Letter template

The best way to get someone in authority to listen to, consider and act on your views is to write a letter to them. Your opinion really can change the world. We suggest sending your ideas, thoughts and concerns about the environment to people 'in power'. This means your local council, the government or the media. This template just reminds you of the important bits of information you need to include.

Your address with postcode, telephone number and email address goes here

The person's full name, their position in the organization and their address with postcode

Date

Title (think of a title or reference that describes what your letter is about)

Dear Mr/Mrs (add surname)

Write your letter here. It is very important to be polite; if you're rude they will throw the letter away or contact you and give you a good telling off!

Sign the letter here with your usual signature

PRINT your full name clearly underneath

Index